They called me the

BRUSH SLINGER

CREATING A CAREER IN ART

Hall Groat Sr.

iUniverse, Inc.
Bloomington

They called me the BRUSH SLINGER
CREATING A CAREER IN ART

iUniverse books may be ordered through booksellers or by contacting:

iUniverse
1663 Liberty Drive
Bloomington, IN 47403
www.iuniverse.com
1-800-Authors (1-800-288-4677)

ISBN: 978-1-4620-7242-2 (sc)
ISBN: 978-1-4620-7243-9 (e)

Printed in the United States of America

iUniverse rev. date: 12/19/2011

TABLE OF CONTENTS

Chapter 2
Corporate Accounts

Chapter 3
Bright Side of My Career

Chapter 4
Dark Side of My Career

Chapter 5
Special Commissions

Chapter 6
Recognition and Awards

Chapter 7
Viewpoints on Art

Chapter 8
Tidbits

REPRODUCTION LIST

Brooklyn Rooftops
36 x 48 in. Oil on canvas by Hall Groat Sr.

Youth Orchestra
16 x 20 in. Oil on panel by Hall Groat Sr.

First Home/Studio, Cazenovia, New York

Francine Butler Groat with husband Professor Hall Groat II,
Hall Sr. and late wife Rosemarie at Groat Sr. exhibition
at Roberson Museum, Binghamton, New York.

Monhegan Moonlight
24 x 48 in. Oil on panel by Hall Groat Sr.

Morning Glory
24 x 24 in. Oil on panel by Hall Groat Sr.

Monhegan Island, Maine
36 x 48 in. Oil on canvas by Hall Groat Sr.

Onondaga Pottery
Historical Painting
By Hall Groat Sr.
Commissioned by Syracuse China Corporation

Dr. Dale Weight, Syracuse Savings Bank CEO, and
Hall Groat Sr. holding scale model of mural.

The Decision
30 x 20 in. Oil on panel by Hall Groat Sr.
1994 Juror's Award
26th Annual Washington and Jefferson National Painting Show

Gordon Steele Memorial Award
12 x 12 in. Oil on canvas by Professor Hall Groat II

New York City Nocturne
41 x 22 in. Oil on panel by Hall Groat Sr.

Provincetown Library
24 x 18 in. Oil on canvas by Hall Groat Sr.

Brooklyn Bridge
33 x 12 in. Oil on canvas by Hall Groat Sr.

Museum School, Clark Institute
24 x 24 in. Oil on panel by Hall Groat Sr.

Rosemarie Groat, Hall Groat Sr. and Priscilla Grauer (sister)
at United Nations ambassador's party in New York City.

Hall Groat in belfry tower with murals in progress at
St. John the Evangelist Church, Syracuse, New York.

New York Stock Exchange
40 x 30 in. Oil on canvas by Hall Groat Sr.

Hall Groat: A Man and His Art
WCNY Public Television Documentary

Barbershop Quartet
By Norman Rockwell
Megalopolis
By Hall Groat Sr.
1962 Berkshire Museum Purchase Prize and Groat at age 29

Maestro Leopold Stokowski summons Hall Groat Sr. to the podium.

Cowboy "Poker Players"
20 x 23 in. Oil on canvas by Hall Groat Sr. (age 15)
Painted over the top of a herd of sheep from circa 1880

Village in Antwerp
21 x 14 in. Watercolor by Hall Groat Sr. (age 16)

The Greenhouse
30 x 40 in. Oil on canvas by Hall Groat Sr.

Lincoln
72 x 48 in. Oil on canvas by Hall Groat Sr.
Collection of Terry Pickard

New York City
30 x 40 in. Oil on canvas by Hall Groat Sr.

The Hindu
24 x 24 in. Oil on panel by Hall Groat Sr.

Amsterdam Drawbridge
24 x 36 in. Oil on panel by Hall Groat Sr.

Air Rescue
70 x 48 in. Oil on canvas by Hall Groat Sr.
Le Cheval, Group Exhibition
Cazenovia College Art Gallery, Reisman Hall

Homestead Remembered
24 x 30 in. Oil on canvas by Hall Groat Sr.

Hall Groat II and Hall Groat Sr. discussing a painting.

FOREWORD

Following his 1959 graduation from the School of Art at Syracuse University, Hall Groat Sr. worked as an illustrator and architectural designer, but found himself ill-suited to the trappings of office life. Instead, he set out on a path to pursue his desire to be a full-time, self-employed artist. Drawing on childhood experiences from the end of the depression that introduced him to the rugged individualism and savvy marketing techniques of the business world, Groat came up with ingenious ways to introduce and sell his art. He reached out to the Central New York business community, which embraced his paintings and murals, and created a niche for his valued impressionist works. For more than half a century, he has sustained his vision of his life as an artist and his works are now found in galleries and collections around the world. In *They Called Me the Brush Slinger: Creating a Career in Art*, Groat chronicles his years in the art world. "For an adventurous young person who wants to be free and interpret the world through the eyes of an artist, it's a life experience you will never regret," Groat writes.

Jay Cox
Editor, *Syracuse University Magazine*

PREFACE

There is something profound about working alone. For nearly fifty years, I have been somewhat reclusive. I have discovered life becomes your own invention, and you're insulated from much of the emotional contagion that confronts your fellow citizens. Alone, with only creative skills to rely on for daily pleasure, presents a challenge. When your creative efforts captivate your full attention, your concern about worldly endeavors becomes irrelevant. Much of what you hear and read about may be deleted unless it concerns your personal family. You stay connected to the world through television and the Internet, although you're not an active player. You learn to take much of the joy and the pain of everyday existence in a philosophical way. An artist communicates through his art and if the work connects with his patrons, it's an achievement. If the artist fails to connect, it may be a dark day. However, when your work also brings self-satisfaction, you may feel a true sense of accomplishment.

In writing these stories, it helps me to understand myself more, and why I entered into such a lonely lifestyle. The only way I can achieve satisfaction is through introspection and immersing myself in my work. Each day the opportunity to create an outstanding work of art offers reassurance—that who I am, and what I do, is worthy of sharing with the world. Many people in my field may harbor similar feelings about their careers, and I find it important for them to know they're not alone. Today, more than any time in modern history, people work at home, and regardless of their profession, many may identify with me.

ACKNOWLEDGMENTS

Somehow it seems that finishing a book is not unlike finishing a painting. It gets harder at the end. Fortunately I have some good friends who would not let me quit.

First I want to thank author and businessman Mel Rubenstein for his advice and countless hours reading my manuscripts.

Attorney Frank Decker was very encouraging by reading the stories and being a troubleshooter when my computer crashed.

Attorney Robert McAllister, an old fraternity brother, has followed my career since high school and proofread my work in progress.

My neighbor George Han was helpful during all my computer problems as well as critiquing my art.

Professor Hall Groat II, artist and publisher who requested I write about my career in the first place, has offered endless technical advice.

A special thanks to my editors Michelle Edgerton and Jay Cox.

They called me the
BRUSH SLINGER
CREATING A CAREER IN ART

THE QUESTION

For many years customers, as well as artists, have asked me the same question: *"How have you maintained a career as a full-time, self-employed artist for over 40 years while no other artist in Central New York has been able to?"* The question is too complex to answer in a few simple words. One thing is for sure, success in art is not just an art contest. There is much more to being an artist and businessman than that. I have met many wonderful artists who envy the fact that I am self-employed while they must have a separate job to exist.

CHAPTER 1

THE EARLY YEARS

AN ATTRACTION TO ART

Growing up in a family where salesmanship was a way of life had a profound effect on my development as an artist. When I was four years old, I can remember my father sending me door-to-door selling quarts of cherries I picked from a small orchard in our backyard. Although I was a natural salesman, I was not yet educated in basic mathematics. I priced the cherries at ten cents a quart and two for a quarter. The concept was flawed and I soon found out the neighbors never opted for the two. Eventually I learned how to set my price and my parents were pleased when my sales increased. My parents believed an early start in business would benefit me in the long term. Later in life, my art replaced the cherries, and those early marketing skills led me to the pathway of success.

When I was about ten years old, my parents surprised me with an oil painting set they hid in my dresser. I was so excited I did my first oil without even removing the box from the drawer by just propping up a canvas board. The painting was of Niagara Falls and I did it from memory after seeing a picture in the library.

Looking at art books in the Petit branch library in Syracuse consumed much of my early youth. I was a lazy reader, but I was able to analyze reproductions and became familiar with color and composition on my own. In my sixth-grade art class at Edward Smith School, I was fortunate to have a teacher who took an interest in my art. Her name was Rhoda Strable and she allowed me to work independently. She was amazed at large seascapes I did from my imagination. She called my mother to inform her I had extraordinary painting skills. My mother proudly hung the paintings from school all over our kitchen walls. Like so many kids in those days, I had paper routes and mowed lawns. I rarely asked my parents for money and took pride in buying some of my own clothing and art supplies. This was not long after the depression and I could see how my parents struggled to support the family.

At twelve years old I was a paperboy. When I came around weekly to collect, I became interested in the original artwork on the walls of customers' homes. When I asked where the art came from, many folks told me a son or daughter in fine arts at Syracuse University did them. When a particular painting appealed to me, I would peer through a window from outside and take a second look. I am sure they thought this was strange and unusual, but my interest in looking at art was unusually strong. With the extra money I saved from my paper route and other odd jobs, I walked to Levine's art store on Crouse Ave. and bought art supplies for painting and to do posters for school. I did many of the school's dance posters later in high school for the HI-Y club and my fraternity Pi-Phi. By concentrating so much on my art, I tuned out the other class work being taught. I was a daydreamer, and haven't changed much in the past sixty-five years.

One day I wandered alone to Jamesville quarry with my sketchpad and pencils and did some remarkable drawings of pine trees and rock formations. To this day, each time I paint rocks and trees I reflect back on that experience at the quarry. The way I sketched them has become indelible in my memory. One time, my older brother Ellery told me he saw an artist working at his easel by Jamesville Reservoir. I begged him to take me out there to watch, but by the time we got there the artist had already left. I was very disappointed.

At one point, my sister and I enrolled in the Saturday art classes for kids at the Syracuse Museum of Fine Arts on the corner of James and State streets. It was the old Everson mansion with creaky floors—although the paintings were gorgeous. There were many WWII paintings in the art room. I was in the watercolor class of Priscilla Burg. She and her twin sister, Prudence, both taught children's art. My sister, Priscilla, was in Prudence Burg's class where soldiers in uniform came to model. Priscilla was very good at drawing, but not everyone has that burning desire to create art. She went on to become a New York fashion model after studying drama at Syracuse University.

One day I was sent to the museum director's office and informed I was wasting too much paper (five cents a sheet) and if I failed to produce a finished painting, I would be expelled from class. The class cost fifty cents a week and four cents for the bus.

When I was in the Cub Scouts, I had to participate in projects that were of interest to me. I began by making rings out of plastic, but it was my cartooning that caught people's eyes. Though I lost interest in being a scout, I enjoyed hiking on my own or with other neighborhood kids. I guess I just didn't enjoy being in a controlled group.

I started skipping school and going to the movies. The first movie I saw was *The Picture of Dorian Gray*. It became a classic and was so memorable it set the stage for my lifetime career as an artist.

My mother was aware of my strong interest in art. She contacted a graduate student, Bud Lancaster, from the Syracuse University School of Art. He came every week and taught me how to do renderings of stars from movie magazines. That was a thrill for me, and I improved quickly. Bud would show me his own drawings of the stars and I was always amazed at how real they looked.

For some reason I didn't get much out of my art class at Nottingham High School. The teacher was too rigid and seemed to dote over the high honor-roll girls. In my last semester there, a substitute teacher took over the class. Joe Gandino was impressed with my watercolor work and gave me a 100 on my report card. The principal, Emmett Kane, told him, "No student is perfect, so make it a 98." That'll work!

I transferred to Central High School and wound up with fellow student Charles Hinman in watercolor class. Central had a better art program than Nottingham. The teachers, Miss Haven and Miss Hueber, gave Charles their undivided attention. Charles went on to become world famous with his stretched canvas designs—even at Central he did great work.

Because I was not getting any individual instruction, my mother found another private teacher, Lee Trimm, who was a strong academic instructor. He came to our house for my first lesson. My father built an easel and placed it in the middle of our living room. It kept falling down until Lee got it stabilized. I was horrified when my whole family sat around to watch as Lee gave his lesson. I was very self-conscious. In retrospect I think it was insensitive of them to sit and gawk at me taking an art lesson.

Having just completed his World War II murals in the Onondaga County War Memorial building in Syracuse, Lee was very confident, all business, and went about his teaching professionally. The lesson consisted of still-life drawing at an easel using charcoal. He used so many construction lines as a way to measure distances from one object to another that, as a result, I developed an angular style that has been with me throughout my career. The follow-up lessons were at his third-story flat on Westcott Street.

I've never had any instructor quite so academic. He showed me his World War II sketchbooks that he carried with him throughout his military service. Lee was a small man and what amazed me was all the figures in his drawings looked like dwarfs. He required I keep a sketchbook, but I never did. Because I ignored his request, he discontinued my weekly lessons that cost five dollars each.

Lee was a top student when he was at Syracuse University, but failed to see my dedication to art. I had a morning paper route and lacked the energy required for evening art class. On my last lesson he gave me an antique oil painting of a herd of sheep that he had picked up somewhere. I painted a picture right over it at home. The subject consisted of cowboys sitting under a tree, playing poker. I still have that painting in my collection.

Word got around I was doing artwork and a boy who lived in the neighborhood came to my door with a WWII fatigue jacket and wanted a picture of a nude painted on the back of it. He paid me five dollars, and this was my first art sale. A woman next door wanted a wall mural in her kitchen depicting Greek dancers. For that she paid me in baklava and other Greek pastries. Her husband owned the Cosmo Restaurant on Marshall Street, where I was offered free lunches throughout my college days. Very often people would come by to have portrait sketches done. For my mother, a tropical fish mural on the bathroom wall was a memorable project she seemed to enjoy.

GIFT OF IMAGINATION

We had a college student rooming at our home on Fellows Ave. I was four and it was the Christmas season. Neal Smith wanted to give me a gift I may someday use. It's the only personal gift I remember receiving from so long ago. It inspired me and stimulated my imagination. I would sit and stare at the gift and never really be sure how to use it. This block of balsa wood was about two feet long and used in the building of models. For years I considered various things to build with it, but no idea seemed feasible. I took small pieces from the balsa block, but never really wanted to destroy it. I just kept it. Our whole family loved Neal Smith and it remained in my possession for many years as a reminder of what a generous and kind person he was.

GIFFORD BEAL'S *FREIGHT YARDS*

At twelve years old I became attached to specific paintings I had seen at the Syracuse Museum of Fine Arts. It seems unusual, as I think back, that certain paintings would draw me to them over and over. The subject matter probably had something to do with it because I have always been fascinated with railroad yards. But just as important as the subject matter was the bold and direct way Gifford Beal painted *Freight Yards*. The billowing smoke that filled the environment gave a sense of excitement as if the artist was just painting it. I felt his sense of urgency by the loaded brush marks that displayed his love of his subject matter. I would categorize it as expressionistic by the uninhibited brush marks that showed a lack of concern about detail. The painting seemed to fit my personality by its understated passages and a certain reckless abandonment. "Let's get the subject down immediately before the feeling leaves or the freight train starts moving away" was the way I read this work. For most of my life I have revisited Beal's *Freight Yards*, and I feel exactly like I'm twelve each time.

Brooklyn Rooftops
36 x 48 in. | Oil on canvas | By Hall Groat Sr.

KNOWING YOUR CUSTOMERS

In 1968 while showing at the Wellfleet Gallery on Cape Cod, I met a family at my opening that stood out from the others. They purchased a group of my paintings and the following year added to their collection. When I asked their names, they turned out to be the son, daughter-in-law and grandchildren of Fleet Admiral of the Navy Chester Nimitz of World War II fame. My new customer was Admiral Chester Nimitz Jr.

Selling art is important to artists in making a livelihood and the awareness of who your buyers are is often equally as important. Unfortunately, many of my early buyers made purchases through galleries that did not supply their names for my records. The galleries are often afraid of their artists working direct. The business can be very cold and self-representing artists have a better opportunity to know and interact with their customers.

HOMAGE TO A CASTLE

I spent time in Korea as a combat rifleman and an occupational soldier. Upon my return home, entering the fine arts program at Syracuse University helped renew my love for the arts. Growing up in the university section, I was familiar with the campus and was always intrigued with the castle on the hill that loomed over the city like a beacon of culture. Yates Castle was unfortunately razed one year prior, but spared was Crouse, a Romanesque Revival castle designed by Archimedes Russell and built in 1881. A few of my art classes were held on the third floor of Crouse, which had a panoramic view of Syracuse and Onondaga Lake. Montague Charman, my watercolor professor, was impressed when I did paintings looking out from the castle windows. He personally encouraged the university to buy my art and in my senior year one of my works was hung in Shaw dormitory.

The music school shared space with the art school in Crouse and this was a great bonus for my education. From the auditorium, organ music, as well as a constant flow of classical works being practiced daily, could be heard throughout the building. Free Sunday concerts were well attended by students and the public. Many students could be seen working on their art while sitting in the auditorium. The music served as inspiration. Walking through the hallways you could hear the piano music from the practice rooms. One day in particular, I stood outside a practice room, listening to a student studying a Bach fugue that he practiced over and over. The door was open and when he spotted me watching for a long while, he motioned for me to come in. He took the time to explain to me the way the work was constructed in seven parts. I had not studied music since I was five years old. I had a German teacher with a heavy accent who I could not understand. She told my mother I showed no ability in piano—I was dropped! And now in college, nearly twenty years later, someone was revitalizing my interest in piano. However, by this time I was into my major and realized I could not recapture the time it would take for piano studies. It's sad—but there may have been a musician in me that was somehow shortchanged. Nevertheless, I at least took a year of music appreciation in Crouse. The opportunity of having classes in Crouse opened my eyes in the world of aesthetics. Studying in Crouse College—which was placed on the National Register of Historic Places in 1974—played an important role in my entire cultural development, and every time I drive around Route 690 or 81 South, the sight of the old castle on the hill brings a smile to my face.

During that time in history, there were several tenured professors who were somewhat antiquated, but still strong academically. Many younger professors had embraced the avant-garde and non-objective art movements in painting. I found in that mix the ideal education that has allowed me to become a complete artist with greater vision and versatility.

Youth Orchestra
16 x 20 in. | Oil on panel | By Hall Groat Sr.

ARMY ART

On New Year's Eve, December 31, 1952, my family had a special surprise for me after I blew out the twenty candles celebrating my birthday. My father, Romaine, who was a joker, had planted an official document under my dinner plate. With great anticipation they watched for my shocked reaction when I opened my "greetings from Uncle Sam." I got drafted! Our country was still in the throes of the Korean War and compulsory military service was in effect. A few days later I reported to the local draft board and was inducted.

Ft. Devens, Massachusetts, was a processing center when I was drafted into the army. In a formation one morning there was an announcement made asking if anyone was an artist or could do a few small murals in the NCO club. One other soldier and I volunteered. We decided to do simple silhouettes on the walls of the club. The subject matter consisted of a drummer and a few other musicians playing. An officer suggested we might stay at Ft. Devens longer and not be sent off to basic training. That sounded encouraging, but proved too good to be true. In two days we were sent out with the rest of the troops to basic at Indian Gap, Pennsylvania.

After four months of basic training I received my orders: I was going to Korea. My embarkation for overseas was going to be from Seattle. The train ride across the USA from Syracuse to Seattle took four days and traveled through the Rocky Mountains. I found them so inspirational I did some sketches from the observation car.

My first several weeks in Korea were spent on the front lines in combat situations. The truce finally came on July 27, 1953, and I was now part of the "occupational" peacetime force. With a few moments to relax, I enjoyed doing watercolor paintings of the mountains, Korean street scenes, and even of the tents in our company area. When my company commander discovered I had skill with paintbrushes he ordered me to make signs for everything, including the Easy Company bulletin board. I also had to letter signs that read, "Latrine Closed." Then he had me paint caricatures of the men to hang on the walls of the mess hall. I soon had to remove them as some nationalities felt discriminated against. The company commander then wanted stripes painted on the helmet liners. There were so many to do I had no free time, so in protest, I threw my paintbrushes away. That wound up being a good idea, because I was issued a pass to Seoul to buy new ones. Going to Seoul was always a good distraction.

With my new brushes, I was ordered to paint a mural in an army mess hall. I had to do it in one night because it had to be ready for an inspection the next morning. I had the brushes, but for this job I needed more paint colors. I got a pass to go back to Seoul to buy the paint. I found out there was no paint store, as we know it. One shop had only three colors available.

When I asked for green, they dumped a muddy color into a bucket of yellow. With that limited supply and a few tubes of paint my sister had sent from home, I began the job. There was no electricity, so a corporal held a kerosene lantern all night so I could get an idea of what I was doing. The next day there was good news and bad news. The good news was we won the title "Best mess hall of the division." The bad news was Virgil Jones, who held that lantern all night, got a "Dear John" letter from his wife saying she was leaving him. He was shattered.

After I was discharged, I returned to Syracuse to manage the family business my mother was running since my father had passed away in April 1953. It wasn't until I talked with professors and art educators from the university who hung out at Pop Welch's bar that I decided to enter the Syracuse University School of Art, and while running the family business, I still received academic honors. My mother soon decided to sell the business, which consisted of the manufacturing and sales of automotive products. She knew my first love was art. After graduation it was difficult to find employment with my major in fine arts illustration. The boom in the photography industry put many illustrators out of business. I went to work for General Electric as a graphic artist for three years, and as a designer at Sergeant, Webster, Crenshaw and Foley architects for two years. Working with architects was certainly more satisfying than working at G.E.; however, I was never completely happy until I became a full-time artist. Being self-employed doing what I love has brought me pure joy for over forty years.

THE TRANSITION FROM SIGN PAINTING TO TWO-DIMENSIONAL PAINTING

It seems strange to think that doing posters in high school and later sign painting to survive would be of such value in my paintings of the future. Composition was difficult when I started painting at a young age. In my quest to be a good sign painter and show-card lettering expert, I found studying layout was mandatory. The nature of most signs and poster art is two-dimensional flat. Becoming good at this work depends on constant practice in layout of copy. Typically a beginner would run out of room doing a long line of lettering in signage. As you practice you develop a better grasp of the negative and positive space and the weight of your letters or designs. Learning how to contrast sizes of copy to create good readability and impact in design is equally as important as the brush skills that must be acquired. Studying how to do professional hand lettering requires an understanding of the value of negative space. Music is written with rests and without them sound runs together and can be irritating to the ear. The same is true in the production of any art form. If you're insensitive to the negative and positive space, you will not be successful. I asked a world-famous watercolorist how he determined which of his paintings were the best. He said, "The ones where I have held the most white paper in the end are my best." That is negative space and is equally as important as the positive. Critiquing my painting in college, German Bauhaus artist Josef Albers told me I had a tendency to be too busy. "Do less and get more," he said.

First Home/Studio, Cazenovia, New York

COOPER DECORATION

Casimir Maciulewicz (Chuck Mack) graduated from the Chicago Institute of Art and was a flamboyant person for whom I worked at Cooper Decoration, a Syracuse company. Although he was temperamental, he had tremendous ability in every phase of art. Cooper's hired high school and college kids for cheap labor and I learned practical things about art that were not offered in my classes.

Harris Cooper, the owner, said to stay in the art department I must become an expert in show-card lettering, because much of the work consisted of booth cards for trade shows. I practiced night and day; however, it wasn't until I met Jack Gaffer, a professional sign painter also working at Cooper's, that I broke through to become a professional. Most all signage was done by hand before the advent of computer graphics. Show-card lettering has become a lost art as the old pros have faded into history.

Because Jack was a heavy drinker, I was puzzled how he could do such perfect lettering when his hand shook so badly. He told me most sign painters are drunks and you learn to do straight lines between the shakes. He knew I wanted to be the best, so he made a deal with me. If I bought a case of beer and worked the entire night in his attic studio on Gifford Street, he guaranteed by morning I would be the best. I was already good, but to be the best was a giant leap. He lined old newspapers across a long, angled drawing table against the wall. By using the columns for guidelines, he drilled me on developing the dash and brush control that makes lettering free and professional. The beer helped him do his flawless demonstrations and after practicing for eight hours straight, and consuming my half of the beer, I must admit I became a pro with near perfect brush control. And although this may sound impossible, perfecting that extraordinary brush control has helped my career in art more than anything else.

Working at Cooper's was fun and we did a wide variety of art-related jobs that were also helpful in my learning to be a painter. A graduate student from Syracuse University and I were assigned to paint a large backdrop for the New York State Fair. When we met, he spelled out his name for me: D-A-V-I-D. He told me it was a beautiful name when pronounced correctly and to never call him Dave. As we painted, he talked about color vibrations in our woodland scenery and other things I had never considered. Working with David was enlightening and we turned out a wonderful theatrical backdrop. He was an eccentric guy—but brilliant. David died in his early thirties of a brain tumor.

Chuck Walkingstick, one of the sign painters at Cooper's, decided to try his hand at painting. He was always broke, but had landed a fat commission for a non-objective painting for Dr. George Bladen of Fayetteville. He laid out a large canvas on the floor at Cooper's and slapped paint all over without having any idea of what he was doing. People laughed at him and told him to stick to his lettering. He then enlisted everyone nearby to walk all over his painting, tracking the colors into a maze. When he thought it looked done he said, "Stop!" When Dr. Bladen saw it, he paid Chuck $500. Chuck had been cynical about modern art and wanted to prove his point. He had the last laugh. He was a Native American from Oklahoma and when I brought him home for lunch one day, my mother said, "You must be *Chief Runningcane*. My son told me you made a nice sale." It was an innocent mistake by my mother and Chuck took it in good humor.

Harris Cooper was shrewd in business and tighter than a tick. He bought tons of WWII surplus material along with thousands of yards of fabrics used for parachutes and numerous military uses. The company used the fabrics for many years to create banners to hang across streets in celebrating events and in decorations for holiday seasons. Buntings and wall décor were also crafted for the inaugural balls and conventions. One time we kids were sketching nudes on the walls at Cooper's. When I did a controversial doodle on the old military Quonset wall, I was summoned over the loudspeaker to the office. When I realized they knew I did the sketch, I thought I was in trouble with the boss. Instead, the art director, Chuck Mack, went on to critique the sketch in a complimentary way and said he could tell my style anywhere. The call to the office was all in fun. Nowhere else would this subtle humor happen, but at this crazy decorating company.

One day Harris Cooper called me to his office and asked, "Why do you smile all the time, Hall?" or some psychologically intrusive question. I had no comment, but realized Harris was very eccentric. He often flew his private airplane to Provincetown for weekends to meet friends. One of my typical assignments was doing booth cards for trade shows. Chuck would hand me a list of eighty different companies and wanted them done quickly. Then Harris would come by and inform me the truck was running and ready to leave for the convention in Washington, D.C. He would repeatedly badger me to do the brush lettering faster because I was holding up the driver, or he would say, "The truck is running so hurry." If you were too slow, you would not last long on the job.

The New York State Fair was one of Cooper's accounts. At the fair, there was a new extra-long campaign trailer for Adlai Stevenson that was freshly painted blue. Chuck Mack had to hand letter the copy in large letters across the sides. He was a pro and it looked great—until it was discovered he spelled "Adlai" as "Adeli." I watched him make the correction in the still tacky paint. It was miraculous how he rubbed out his misspelling and made the correction. Stevenson lost the election, so I don't think it mattered much.

While a student of painting at Syracuse University, I was criticized by my professor, George Vander Sluis, for working at Cooper's after class. He told me it would ruin my art. I don't think George realized I was brought up loving production and it was a way of life for me.

In his painting classes, I was always the first one done with my painting. He would make a comment when I started working, but by the time he got around the room once or twice, I was finished. Fellow students called me "A Great Brush Slinger."

PRISCILLA'S GALLERY

In the 1970s my sister, Priscilla, opened her own art gallery in Port Washington, New York. She married on her nineteenth birthday and upon turning forty was ready to take on a new venture in life. She now had three grown boys and, with husband Herman, loved boating. The location of the gallery was a former boathouse supply store close to the marina—an ideal choice. Being across from a famous restaurant brought many visitors to Priscilla's Gallery. She worked hard and found the new direction in life exhilarating. Her sales were brisk, although the cost of doing business was staggering. Her openings were well attended and she was clever at selecting themes that attracted many people. *Five Paintings by Five Men* was a sales success I was part of. In the beginning the gallery would be filled with her personal friends, but soon she developed new customers. One couple sailed over to Port Washington from Connecticut for her opening. The gallery was in business for several years until my sister wanted to devote more time to her poetry and creative writing.

MARBLE SCULPTURE

During the 1980s I took on an additional art form that was a diversion from my long painting career. I purchased a pneumatic chisel and carved many relief sculptures. Most of the work was on bluestone, but some was on Vermont marble from the quarry at Granby. The most outstanding work was created for the Peter Hubbards of Cazenovia. A triptych of unusual trees was the subject of this stone relief and mounted on an interior wall. The Lynns of Skaneateles commissioned a large relief sculpture that I mounted over the entranceway of their lake home. The subject was a large rose created in a contemporary style. Merrill Lynch also commissioned a relief carving of its corporate identity bull. My son, Hall, carved a diptych of two bald eagles for the entranceway to our home. He also sculpted some birdbaths for his mother's garden. After several years our painting careers became too demanding and we abandoned doing the stone sculpture.

ART WORKSHOPS

Art Zimmer is a longtime friend and one of Central New York's leading businessmen. Art is an avid skier and owned a resort hotel at Pico Peak, as well as one in Mt. Snow, Vermont. Art invited me to conduct a summer art workshop at his resorts that proved to be an enjoyable event for my whole family. At the end of each day of painting in the mountains of Vermont, I did a critique on the students' work. My son enrolled in my workshops, which made it special for me. During the winter months we also enjoyed skiing at Pico Peak, Killington and Mt. Snow. It was my source of inspiration for many mountain skiing paintings.

Francine Butler Groat with husband Professor Hall Groat II,
Hall Sr. and late wife Rosemarie at
Groat Sr. exhibition at Roberson Museum, Binghamton, New York.

AGWAY

Before I made the leap into self-employment as an artist, a close friend introduced me to an Agway executive who took an interest in my work. A series of small landscape paintings was ordered and used for business gifts. It was a good decision to accept this commission, as it led to many larger sales in years to come. In building a career it's important to take care of all customers whether orders are small or major projects. Your reputation is all about customer relations and if you slight a client, it may come back to haunt you later in your career.

Monhegan Moonlight
24 x 48 in. | Oil on panel | By Hall Groat Sr.

HANGING PAINTINGS IN A TREE BROUGHT FRUITFUL REWARDS

Living in Lanesboro, Massachusetts, in the Berkshires for a year, I wanted to take advantage of the tourist traffic on Route 7. I had not yet begun my full-time career as a fine artist, but at twenty-nine I had innovative ideas on promotion. Living in a 150-year-old farmhouse set back from the road offered an opportunity to sell my paintings. One day I decided to hang a few large paintings in a tree in front of the house. Although few people stopped, they at least took notice, and that visibility led to some sales and awards in the Berkshires. When you're new in a very old and staid New England town, it could take a hundred years before you're recognized. In my case, it took less than one year. The seemingly goofy idea of hanging art in a tree was instrumental in creating instant exposure that brought fruitful rewards. Sometimes it's better to do anything rather than nothing in fear of looking foolish.

YOUNG MAN'S PAINTING OF HIS MOTHER

When my phone rang one evening, it was a young man with a story that took place many years prior. He told me of his mother's passing some years back and that she had left him with her portrait painted by me. I didn't know his mother well, but she had asked me to do a watercolor portrait study of her just for fun. I hardly remembered this isolated incident, but when the young man offered to show it to me, I was pleased with the quality of the work. It's interesting to look back to an earlier time in your career to track your development as a painter. He said, "My mom always loved the painting and it is my only picture of her and the only way I can remember her. Thanks, sir." I noticed a tear in his eye and realized I had created art that brought great joy to someone. Even though I just painted it for fun, I was rewarded by the pleasant experience of witnessing the power of art and how it can help bond people together. This young man had been estranged from his mother for many years. The painting served as a way for him to reflect on his boyhood life and remember his mother forever.

TELEVISION AND ART

When television was first introduced in Syracuse, people crowded around a department store window on Salina Street, gazing at this eight-inch fuzzy screen in a box called television.

It all seemed like magic and this was before the advent of color TV. Somehow my father scraped together enough money to buy one. It marked the end of sitting around the living room listening to radio, and the end of using your imagination. We watched all the popular programs and sporting events, like the Joe Louis-Billy Conn title fight and the Gonzalez-Segura tennis championship. The world changed overnight. Syracuse University set up its own educational station, and my high school art teacher informed the class that the university was inviting a few students to be the first to be videoed while painting. She asked for volunteers, but most kids were uncomfortable with this idea. I somehow mustered up the courage and found it to be exciting. Little did I know that I would be a guest artist on many local TV shows for years to come. That early exposure on television played an important role in my art career.

PAINTING ON THE WHARF IN PROVINCETOWN

For years, I painted in Provincetown, Cape Cod, in the off-season. People who love P-town go off-season to avoid tourists. One time I set up my easel at the end of a wharf and did a successful series of studies on illustration board. These vignettes were some of my best works and several were sold in New York City. Working on location brings out your best efforts when you're enthralled over the subject matter. Unfortunately, this wharf became a victim of a storm and no longer exists.

SAME-SEX COUPLES

It was a nice drive from South Wellfleet out to Herring Cove Beach on that spring morning in May. My wife and I had our bikes and enjoyed riding the dune trails that led out to the coast guard station. I took some pictures of dune brambles for reference material for my art. Painting on location is better, but impractical on a short getaway when you need to conserve time to see everything. Driving back down Bradford Street, we could see a crowd gathering while looking down a side street toward the town wharf. Out of curiosity we headed back up Commercial Street to check out the action. We parked our car in the town lot and hit some shops. There were gay rights and lesbian activities along the narrow streets. Men were embracing and the public display of homosexuality was more open than usual—even for Provincetown. After lunch at our favorite restaurant, we walked toward the courthouse. There were hundreds of same-sex couples waiting in long lines to exchange their vows. Along the sidewalks were parents, siblings and relatives of the happy couples. We overheard gay men and lesbian couples introducing their new partners to mom and dad. After each couple was joined in wedlock, a loud cheer of joy was heard and the confetti flew. The general atmosphere was one of love, or at least acceptance, by most families. It was May 17, 2004—a day that made history in the Commonwealth of Massachusetts. Emotions were high in this town that has been a center for same-sex couples since the Portuguese fishermen and the Pilgrims landed on Cape Cod.

SHIFTING DUNES

Hiking through the dunes looking for the perfect subject for a dune painting is an exercise in futility. There is no such thing, and I finally realized the wind and surf waters sculpt infinite shapes that are never duplicated in nature. It was then that I became a painter, with the wisdom of knowing that any composition I could possibly dream up would already exist in the infinite possibilities of nature.

DR. EGAN'S TOOTH

When we moved to Manlius a group of kids came by our garage to meet my kids. Some asked about the paintings I was unloading. One of the eight-year-olds told me his dad was a dentist. I don't know what possessed me, but I asked him to go home and ask his dad for a tooth so I could do a painting of it. Sure enough, he returned with a large molar with several fillings in it. Since the dentist had taken me seriously, I went ahead with a small painting of it. I gave it to the doctor's kids to bring home. What I thought to be a silly joke turned out to be the opposite. Dr. Egan and his wife had the tooth painting framed and it was one of their favorite small works. Since that day they have collected many of my paintings for their homes as well as for the dental office.

MISTAKEN IDENTITY

One summer at a cocktail party in Cazenovia at the home of an old friend and customer of mine, there was a large group sitting in the living room. A couple entered who I hadn't met before. They were so elated to finally meet me that they went right up to my family doctor saying, "It's so nice to meet you in person after seeing all your work, Hall." The doctor was dressed exactly as you would expect an artist to look. He was wearing a casual black outfit with no tie and had a long ponytail and a goatee. I was sitting nearby him, but without the image they expected of an artist. The doctor then introduced them to me as the artist. I detected embarrassment in the couple and there was little conversation to follow this mistaken identity.

THE DISINGENUOUS COUPLE

While living on Tuscarora Lake in Erieville in my mid-thirties, I received an early Sunday morning phone call from a couple living in Cazenovia. They were anxious to buy some paintings from me and asked if I could bring a selection over that morning. It was an odd hour for them to call and make such a request, but they sounded serious about it, so I agreed. They wanted me to set the paintings around their gorgeous living quarters while they stuffed down donuts and coffee. They discussed my art in their pseudo-philosophical attempt to impress me. The couple consumed more donuts and coffee and they seemed to have no regard for my time. Finally, after two hours, they showed me to the door, but had never hinted at buying a thing. It became apparent I was being used for the entertainment of this disingenuous couple. It may have been a case of a husband wanting to impress his new young wife, and the couple was divorced soon after.

THE NEIGHBOR

Twenty years ago my son and I were doing an art workshop at Whiteface Mountain in the Adirondacks. An elderly gentleman was hanging out while his wife was in my workshop. Making small talk, I asked him where he was from. When he said Syracuse, New York, I asked him what street he lived on. He answered, "505 Fellows Avenue." Much to his surprise, I informed him I knew his mother's name was Daisy Quinn. He was amazed when I asked if his dad practiced lacrosse in their backyard with a man named Romaine. He replied, "Yes, how did you know that?" I answered, "Because I was your next-door neighbor, Mr. Quinn."

Quinn didn't remember me, as I was only four years old at the time, but he did remember his dad and my father playing lacrosse in their backyard. Thanks to my art career I got the chance to reminisce with someone who knew my father.

PUTTING THE AUDIENCE TO SLEEP

When I was living in the Berkshires, I was invited by the Adams Art League to do a slide presentation of my paintings. The lights were turned down so the art enthusiasts could see the images of my work while I talked. They were very polite people and listened intently—or so I thought. Soon I could hear the faint sounds of snoring that grew louder as I went on. When I finished I turned off the projector and on with the lights. I asked if anyone had questions. There was no reply, as I had put most people to sleep. It may have been the thin air by Greylock Mountain that contributed to their drowsiness, or it could have been my presentation. I will never know for sure.

LOLA'S A MOHAWK FROM ST. REGIS

One student who made teaching fun was Lola. On her first class she addressed me as Mr. Groat. I asked her several times to call me Hall, as I didn't require formality with my private students.

One day she called me "Chief" and has addressed me that way for over twenty years. Lola's a Mohawk from St. Regis in northern New York. Calling me "Chief" was a respectful name designation and is one I still enjoy. Unlike other students, Lola always had a special plan for each painting completed during the session. Being a generous person, she loved to honor friends with her paintings. The last work she gifted was to the owner of the club where she played golf to hang in the restaurant. Many times she would arrive with a pound of candy, knowing it was one of my weaknesses. Lola was a hardworking student who set up a studio in her home to improve her art by practicing daily. To this day, her work is colorful and projects her flamboyant personality. When my phone rings and I hear "Hi, Chief," it has a very endearing sound and can only be Lola.

A PUDDLE IN TOWN CAN BE A SEASHORE IN A PAINTING

Looking for a nautical subject would seem ridiculous when you're in a residential area in Syracuse—but don't bet on it. A few blocks from my old homestead on Miles Ave. the subject matter I wanted to paint, "the seashore," revealed itself. No, I wasn't delusional. It had been raining a few days before and a neighbor had parked his fishing boat in his driveway. There was a puddle next to the boat that became a reflection pool. As I painted the boat its reflection appeared exactly as if it was by the seashore. If you're too literal about the selection of subject matter, you may miss out on the way you can interpret the world around you. No—there was no seashore there in reality. But to be sure, it was every bit a seashore in the painting. To find the perfect subject matter an artist must develop acute environmental awareness.

SUNDAY MORNING OFFICE HOURS

Dr. Herbert Katz, ophthalmologist, was a collector of fine art and oriental rugs. His wife had passed on and he kept busy in his advancing years. His secretary called me periodically and requested I bring in an assortment of art for Sunday morning. When I arrived at his office in the Medical Arts Building, there would be several patients waiting to see him. He always ushered me in first and showed me his collection of Orientals and paintings by Edna Hibel. Then he would buy a selection of my work. We both loved to talk about art, but I doubt his patients enjoyed the wait.

Morning Glory
24 x 24 in. | Oil on panel | By Hall Groat Sr.

FIRST SYMPHONY

The first symphony I attended while a youth was at Lincoln auditorium in Central High School. An elderly woman who I did work for was ill and gave me her ticket. It was an orchestra seat and Van Cliburn was performing my favorite: *Symphony No. 2* by Rachmaninoff. I was hooked on symphonic music from that day on. While living in the Berkshires in 1962, I would frequent Tanglewood to hear the Boston Symphony. Now I feel extraordinarily fortunate to live in a city with the Syracuse Symphony Orchestra so accessible.

GROWING UP WITH ART

As a young child, living in a home full of art during those impressionable years is important. I have found it amazing the way my second generation of art buyers remember my paintings that surrounded them as kids. They are able to recollect in such detail that I know I have connected with them. A great many of my customers who downsize their homes find happy recipients for their art collections in their children and grandchildren. One of my customers, who had moved to Florida with her eight children, told me her kids had been arguing over her paintings because many want the same ones. She came up to my studio and we selected a new group of paintings to satisfy them all.

In my home growing up, we had oils by my grandfather and uncle who were both amateur painters. My mother also purchased abstract work and rotated our collection so we could be exposed to a variety of styles, from conservative to contemporary. Sometimes my grandfather's and uncle's work rotated to the attic until they called to say they were coming for a visit. She then scrambled to have some of them hanging again.

CHAPTER 2

CORPORATE ACCOUNTS

NIAGARA MOHAWK

One of my portrait commissions for Niagara Mohawk Power Corp. was for a building dedication. The painting in memory of a beloved executive was an elaborate event. I was supplied with photo references and the oil painting was to be approved by a committee for the posthumous honor. The committee never agreed on whether the subject was bald, or just had a little dark hair on the sides, or a full head of hair that was white, or if it was black. The reference photo did not correspond with their recollections. I had to do many revisions and finally the work was approved with a little thin hair on top and dark brown with some gray mixed on the sides. The executive's family sent me a letter of appreciation, so I presume I hit the nail on the head—or at least the right hairdo. During my years of creating montage portraits for NIMO and National Grid, I had the honor of painting several CEOs, including John Hale, Bill Donlan, Bill Davis, John Endries, and many other retiring executives.

Many years later I realized if I wanted my career as an artist to move ahead, I would need to find a unique way of doing business. Everyone wonders what goes on inside the corporations that make up our free enterprise system. I decided to launch a program in Central New York that would put me on the inside of our greatest industries. I called several prominent CEOs, requesting tours of their plants. I asked for an appointment to introduce myself and take pictures that would serve as reference for the preparation of artwork that would highlight their operations. Sometimes I was shuffled over to a vice president or a public relations director; however, I was always invited to come in. I always dressed in the appropriate attire and expressed a sincere interest in their corporation. I found I was accorded respect as an artist. During the sixties, executives had less interest in artists, unless they were promoted by Madison Avenue galleries. However, I was an independent artist who shared many of the conservative values of business community leaders.

Being invited on tours to record company operations was truly inspirational to me because I grew up in a family business where streamlining production was the key to success. After most tours, companies expressed an interest in seeing my impression of their workplaces and from that point on I realized business acumen was essential. It's impossible to list all the companies that became my customers, but a large group was instrumental in assuring my self-employment status would take me on a thirty-five year ride of success.

Monhegan Island, Maine
36 x 48 in. | Oil on canvas | By Hall Groat Sr.

BRISTOL LABORATORIES

This tour brought me a commission to create a twenty-six-foot montage mural for the reception area in Building No. 22 on Thompson Road, East Syracuse. It was early in my career and I was very inspired by their products and extraordinary research department. My guide explained the dramatic advancements in the manufacturing of pharmaceutical products that Bristol Laboratories specialized in. The montage mural was painted on stretched canvas in the Canal Barn, where I maintained a second studio for two years. It was then hung on a large wall in the reception area. The majority of my painting career was either done on location or at my home studio.

SYRACUSE SYMPHONY ORCHESTRA

One summer at Green Lakes, I watched an outdoor performance of the Syracuse Symphony Pops Orchestra, directed by Fabio Machetti. It inspired me to later create a small mural in the SSO office. At the urging of Kay Fey, executive secretary, I began working entirely from memory, using no reference material. This resulted in a very impressionistic painting that captured the feeling of the symphony performing rather than any specific detail. A work of art like this can be very difficult, as you have no clear path to completion and must rely on how the painting *feels* as well as looks. Melissa Washington, SSO developmental coordinator, was working at a desk behind me and often seemed mesmerized by the progress. She offered words of encouragement as I struggled to pull it together. At the end of a weekend's work, Trey Devey, executive director, took a look and said, "It's finished!" A work like this is very illusive and the last brush stroke is critical. When working so close to a painting in a small office in the Civic Center, I was not able to view the painting from a distance, therefore the feedback helped. "It's finished!" was a perfectly timed and correct comment.

BRISTOL-MYERS SQUIBB

The head biochemist conducted this tour, which was centered in the research and development area. Coincidently, Dr. Richard Elander, my former neighbor, was my guide. Richard was world famous in his field and authored many books on biochemistry. He introduced me to Pam McGarry, executive secretary, who invited me to take over a longtime art rental program that consisted of original art for the hallways of the executive headquarters. The company decided it wanted a new look.

Being an art collector, I had amassed a sizable collection of local and international artists. Originally, the rental program consisted of art on consignment by local artists. I did not want to be responsible for other artists' work, so I personally owned all works that were hung. The first exhibit was so well received by employees in the executive headquarters that I made some suggestions that would double the size of the rental program. That program would now bring paintings to the inner offices and allow personal selections to be made by the executives themselves. This, in itself, proved to be an incredible improvement. All work was on a six-month lease/purchase agreement, with a 10 percent discount for employees who wanted to purchase art. That virtually turned the program into my gallery, as I had to replace many works that were sold with new works. The program expanded steadily for eight years until the merger with Squibb Company. It was phased out as company downsizing took place and Squibb exerted more control. It was the end of the road for many loyal Bristol employees and the end of one of my most enjoyable and financially successful ventures.

MONTREAL ART COLLECTORS

During the 1970s I often had a Montreal couple come to my studio to select paintings for their gallery. Anita made the picks while Joe walked their dog outside. They were very professional and always looked at canvases strewn across my studio showroom floor. When Anita finished making her selections, she would call Joe in for his approval. Price was all they cared about as they were middlemen and wanted to assure a good profit. They had their own framing business and I'm sure had a huge mark-up. They would roll the work up and drive off in their Cadillac for another artist's studio. Montreal is a very sophisticated city and they enjoyed a large customer base.

MILLER BREWING COMPANY

Gerry Church, resident manager, personally took me through the brewery in Fulton and explained every aspect of the brewing process from fermentation to bottling, canning, packaging, and right out to shipping. We had lunch in the cafeteria, where he showed me a wall he wanted a mural on. It doesn't get any better than that in the art business. The mural consisted of a maze of beer bottles and cans winding through the assembly lines, which was inspired by my tour of the plant. The brewery took on eighty of my original paintings over the next nine years. Many were acquired through a lease/purchase agreement that made it easier for the company to manage the deal. I made frequent trips to Miller and personally hung the work in all the executive offices. Of course, I was always a guest at the outstanding cafeteria while I worked there. One of the final projects for Miller was a 20-foot-high diptych painting of two beer cans right in the canning plant. Soon after that Miller closed the Fulton brewery, bringing an end to a wonderful business relationship.

SYRACUSE CHINA CORPORATION

Chuck Goodman, president of the Syracuse China Corporation, was a neighbor of mine in Manlius. When I visited the plant he made sure I had a deluxe tour. I saw its artists at work creating an identity pattern for a hotel chain that was going to use its china. The history of this business was fascinating and there were many ties to old families. Although I was familiar with the company, it was still a rewarding experience to be taken on an in-depth tour. Bob Theis, the CEO, was an old tennis singles opponent of mine. For my first project, he decided on a painting of how the company looked more than a century ago. Historical themes have always fascinated me. The china company acquired a large selection of my works and honored me by using a reproduction of one of my Syracuse Symphony paintings on plates that were used as favors at a symphony ball, as well as a few complimentary sets that I was given.

Onondaga Pottery
Historical Painting by Hall Groat Sr.
Commissioned by Syracuse China Corporation

MERRILL LYNCH

Karl Smith managed the Syracuse and Binghamton offices of the Merrill Lynch brokerage house. When I met Karl, he was interested in my artwork and collected many paintings for both locations. He took an interest in my career and enjoyed having original paintings hung throughout the buildings. WCNY public television directors approached Karl on his willingness to be interviewed for a documentary on my art career. He was very receptive and conducted an in-depth tour of my art that was presented on TV. Karl often took business associates and investors on talking tours of my paintings as well. Of all my corporate collectors, he displayed the sophistication that you would expect of a museum director. It became apparent to me that his liberal arts education gave him the ability to articulate the importance of my art in relationship to the investment world. Karl was also the Syracuse Symphony Orchestra board president in 1993–94. Our business relationship lasted for many years, until he moved out west and retired.

BOND SCHOENECK & KING

I was awarded a painting commission for a commemorative work of art celebrating the 150th anniversary of this distinguished law firm. I met George Bond II in Cazenovia twenty years earlier when he visited my studio. Now I had to put all the original managing partners from the firm's conception into a montage painting. The law office had previously taken on many of my paintings, so I was already familiar with the firm. The commission was an honor for me, although it was very complex. This particular work was a gift of the Young Agency.

THE YOUNG AGENCY

In mid-career I was commissioned by the Young Agency to do a painting of its building. Ten years later the agency moved to a new location and wanted that added to the painting. Finally the agency wanted the painting to incorporate its entire history and show all of its locations in Syracuse. The painting created an interesting focal point in the reception area and a way of introducing the long heritage of the agency.

SYRACUSE SAVINGS BANK

In 1976 I had been playing too much tennis, which resulted in severe back pain. Dr. Laurie ordered me to bed for ten days, although it's a remedy no longer prescribed by neurosurgeons.

I had previously prepared a mural proposal for an Armory Square restaurant owned by attorney Robert Lawler and his partner. That deal fell through, as the restaurant didn't get off the ground. Knowing this mural would be good for the city, I was determined to find a home for it.

During that time of bed rest I used the phone to continue with my business. Dick Case, a staff reporter of *The Post-Standard*, wrote an article with the caption, "Want a 30-foot mural?" A staff photographer was sent to my home to shoot a picture of this painting. I had just completed my ten days in the sack and had to dress quickly, hobble out to the living room, and try to look alive. The next day my phone rang off the wall with many inquiries on this painting. There were many serious potential corporate buyers, but Dale Weight was my first choice. I had previously sold my large work *Bessemer* to the Syracuse Savings Bank branch in Mattydale through my friend Doc Schwartz, the bank's senior vice president. He discovered the painting at the Associated Artists Gallery.

When I showed Dale the painting he loved it, but said he needed it in a vertical format—my work was horizontal. I told him I would section it off in measurement and do seven scale models to fit the bank lobby. He then asked the impossible, "Hall, can you have them ready by 7:30 a.m. tomorrow with your written proposal and I'll present them at our board meeting." I rushed home and laid out the project in my studio as in a production line, economizing every valuable minute. After spending the entire night with no sleep, I arrived at Dale's office five minutes early. He asked me to sit in his office while he pitched the mural project to the board.

The approval was swift and unanimous. The bank's attorney drew up a contract that seemed very favorable to me as they wanted to buy all of the work I did the previous evening and my original scale model as well. The murals were painted in the bank lobby so the bank had to free up space for a temporary studio. Dr. Weight wanted the public to watch my progress, believing it was a good public relations event. My artist friend, Paul Parpard, stretched the 11-by-6-foot canvas on custom built wooden bars and primed all seven. The frames were designed and milled by PB&H Moulding Company that was nearing its 100th year in business. The bank has changed owners several times since; however, the National Register of Historic Places protects the building. It now houses a permanent one-man exhibition of my work at The Bank of America, 1 Clinton Square.

Dr. Dale Weight, Syracuse Savings Bank CEO, and
Hall Groat Sr. holding scale model of mural.

SKANEATELES SAVINGS BANK

Twenty-five years ago I approached Burdett Lee, president of Skaneateles Savings Bank, about the concept of a mural in his bank. My work consisted of the historical edifices of the town with the old railroad, and the lake behind with the tour boat that still exists today. Mr. Lee told me his ancestors started the harvesting of teasel plants, so this subject played a significant part in the painting. An elderly woman who once was the teacher in the one-room schoolhouse on West Lake Road pressed hard to have her school included. The painting came out well and although the bank has changed hands three times, it still looks as fresh as the day it was painted.

BLUE CROSS/BLUE SHIELD

Charles Lapham, Blue Cross/Blue Shield CEO, with artist wife Marian, a noted water colorist, visited my studio twenty years ago to acquire one of my new abstract acrylics, *Moon Rocks*. This 4-by-6-foot work was their choice for the reception area of the health care company's renovated building. They continued to add more of my work to their collection until Charles retired. Albert Antonini took the helm and also continued collecting my art.

When major additions and renovations were taking place in ten floors of offices, Albert called me in for suggestions on how to designate where paintings should hang. I suggested he use a major painting opposite each elevator landing to designate each floor. By using ten different nature scenes, the employees would easily recognize their floor. We made a deal and I started the work in my garage in Manlius. Al and his vice president came out to see my progress. I lined the work along a hedgerow of arborvitae, as it was the only way they could visualize the whole series. As my neighbors drove by, I noticed a lot of rubber-necking. After approval we trucked the 10 paintings down to the offices and I personally hung them. Al also commissioned a large montage depicting all of the building locations in the history of Blue Cross/Blue Shield. A reception of the newly renovated building highlighting my paintings was a memorable event.

Blue Cross/Blue Shield received a gift of a large painting of Syracuse for its new reception area, which was presented by bank president Jack Webb. I had done this painting on commission years before. The company has since moved into the old Agway building near Shoppingtown Mall in DeWitt.

THE MERRILL TRUST COMPANY

Turning failure into a dream deal was a shining moment in my career. The Merrill Trust Company called me from Bangor, Maine, to submit a scale model of a mural for a new branch bank. They gave me a thousand dollars and full expenses to fly up and present my design to the board. Unbeknownst to me, a local artist residing in Bangor was a shoe-in. He was very good and well-connected in town. As expected, he won the competition and was being awarded the commission—but his ego was his downfall.

A friend of mine headed the architectural office of Sergeant, Webster, Crenshaw & Foley— the firm's satellite office in Bangor. He informed me through the grapevine that the local artist refused to make a revision to his design at the request of the bank's CEO. With nothing to lose, I made a last-ditch effort to get my foot back in the door. Knowing that bankers know little about mural proposals, I called the Merrill Trust president and accused the bank of using unethical practices. My catchword was "unethical." I asked why the winning artist was allowed to do a revision to his painting and I was not extended the same courtesy. He sounded flustered and didn't have a good reason, but said he would call me right back. The vice president of the bank called me back and said they indeed would like a small revision done in my painting and invited me back to present my work again. The bank attorney drew up a contract and I was awarded the full-expenses-paid dream deal.

SCOLARO SHULMAN LAW FIRM

Dick Scolaro and Barry Shulman are well-known attorneys. They both have a love for fine arts and music. Barry is also a professional dance choreographer and respected in the theater. The firm has purchased many of my paintings and has a large work displayed in its boardroom. The works they have selected are contemporary and represent my signature style from the 1980s. I enjoy visiting their offices periodically to review their paintings.

MILTON A. HILL

Milton has a large collection of my work that comprises my mid-career. I also did a painting of Milt fly-fishing that was a surprise for him. His art collection has a wide variety of subjects and techniques. When WCNY public television did a documentary on my career entitled, *Hall Groat: A Man and His Art*, he allowed the TV crew to film his collection of my work and agreed to a personal interview.

GRIMALDI & NELKIN

When you visited the accounting firm's former suite of offices on Catherine Street, you felt like you were in a "Groat Museum." Most of the paintings I did for Ray Grimaldi are 30 by 40 inches and diverse in color and subject. Ray's favorite painting is the first one he collected twenty-five years ago of a regatta—it's a very impressionistic work. Ray's a sportsman and a former gymnast at Syracuse University, and I've noticed he leans more toward the action scenes.

RUDIN MENTER TRIVELPIECE

In the early part of my career, I sold some work to the Trivelpiece family. In more recent times I worked with senior partner, Peter Hubbard. He invited me in to see his new suite of offices in the Seven Hundred Building that he wanted to decorate with art. We talked about his idea of having a theme about the history of Central New York. Peter and wife Hanna previously had me do a major installation of art in their home in DeWitt. He had very definite ideas about the color and subject matter of the paintings he wanted in the offices and conference rooms and that was helpful to me. This was an enjoyable project and Peter and I enjoyed the business side of it as well. When the firm had a photo taken of all the partners, I was flattered to be invited to join them in the picture. The law partners commented that many people were amused to find that I looked as though I could be one of the firm's lawyers.

The Decision
30 x 20 in. | Oil on panel | By Hall Groat Sr.
1994 Juror's Award
26th Annual Washington and Jefferson National Painting Show

LYNN LAW FIRM

The Lynn family has collected my artwork as far back as I can remember. What I find unique about their art collection is the variety of subjects. It seems important to Bill Lynn to represent a full cross section of my work. If I bring a painting to his office he doesn't care for, he is quick to let me know. I enjoy a person who is upfront and honest. The rapport I have developed with this law firm makes being an artist a pleasure. One of its last acquisitions was an imaginary painting I did of the interior of a great museum showing all of my paintings on the wall. That large work is in Bill Lynn's private office. It was also a pleasure to paint an oil of Digby, the family's last Irish wolfhound, depicted playing near the Skaneateles lakefront.

NORTHWESTERN MUTUAL

When Mary Julian, director of the Central New York group's financial network, walked me through its offices in East Syracuse and showed me the colorful art in the hallways, I was puzzled just how my work might fit in. After meeting Paul Dodd, managing partner, I realized my work was to go in the reception area. My work was based on the history of Syracuse and the company wanted to welcome out-of-town clients with the flavor of Syracuse. My 30-by-40 inch painting, *Dome City,* was a perfect fit and it is an honor to be featured in the lobby.

CHAPTER 3

BRIGHT SIDE OF MY CAREER

WELLFLEET ON VIA MIZNER

Palm Beach's Worth Avenue was filled with flower shops and art galleries. As my wife and I went in and out of them, we hit upon the Wellfleet Gallery on Via Mizner that was set back off Worth Avenue. They handled my kind of art. Thomas Gaglione, the director, asked to see my work and I told him I would bring a couple of pieces in the next day. We went back to our beach house where I had some art supplies and I painted a pair of gems. We went to a frame shop and bought two take-off frames. The next day I brought in the work.

Admiral Chester Nimitz Jr., whose father was the WWII Fleet Admiral of the Navy, was my first customer. During the winter season Tom ordered and sold many more of my paintings. *The Palm Beach Social Pictorial* published stories concerning my career.

The following spring I delivered new work to his Wellfleet Gallery on Cape Cod. Tom had a great stable of artists, including such established painters as Xavier Gonzalez and wife Ethel Edwards, Umberto Romano, and Edwin Dickinson. This made space a problem. A new kid on the block didn't get the same exposure as the old pros; however, I made sales because customers love to hunt for up-and-coming artists.

At season's end, Tom was busy crating up his established artists' work when I popped in. I was hurt he was leaving me out, but he explained shipping was too expensive and he could not handle my paintings at Palm Beach. When I saw he needed help I offered to give him a hand packing the wooden crates. I knew Tom was a meticulous man and he wanted the crates to look impressive. I told him I was a professional with a lettering brush, but I had to leave to take my wife to Herring Cove Beach in Provincetown. As I started for the door Tom said, "Wait! I've got a deal for you. If you address my crates, I'll put your work in the boxes for the gallery." I had the job done in no time flat and headed for the beach. The Palm Beach gallery didn't survive for many years, but I exhibited at Wellfleet for ten years. His last words to me after I took him to dinner at the Whitman House were, "I hope I did a good job for you, Hall. I sold 110 of your paintings, more than any other artist in my two galleries."

One of the better openings at Tom's gallery was a group show where I was exhibiting with Edwin Dickinson. Edwin was very old and quite fastidious and insisted on using his own personal wine glass. He was the son of a minister from Seneca Falls, New York. In his advancing years, he was short on patience, but not short of extraordinary art ability. Mrs. Dickinson was very charming. She and Tom apologized to me for her husband's vulgar response to a simple question I asked him about my art in the show. I told them he was straightforward with me and no apology was necessary. In fact, he gave me some good advice and I appreciated his candor. I'm now about the age he was at that time and I'm getting a little ornery too.

Tom certainly ran a professional gallery and always treated my family well. He was an honest man and always paid his artists promptly. Somehow I wish my painting professor at Syracuse University was alive to see why I also worked at the Cooper Decoration Company during my college days.

OEHLAEGER'S GALLERY

Frank Oehlaeger had the best gallery on St. Armands Circle in Sarasota, and I wanted in. I had previously met the Oehlaegers at my one-man show at the Sarasota Art Association, so he was aware of my work. One day I pulled into his driveway behind the gallery and set out a group of paintings I wanted to show him. I decided against calling him first, as he tended to be the type who would play the "I'm too busy game." I wanted to cut through the protocol because we were on a short family trip and there was no time to make an appointment.

As luck had it, Frank and his trophy wife were entering the rear driveway when she burst out, "Oh Frank, I'm so glad you asked Hall to bring in his work. Wow, I love these new works, Hall." By his expression I could tell he didn't share her sentiments; nevertheless, he asked me to bring the work into the gallery. He put my work upstairs with his second stringers, which was less than flattering. He was in the process of installing the Edna Hibel show. He admitted to me he didn't care for her work that tended to be too saccharine, but, with her incredible following, couldn't resist the money.

Frank had a close alliance with Foster Harmon's Gallery in Naples, Florida. They alternated shows with the high-end art. Julio de Diego, artist and jewelry maker (one of Gypsy Rose Lee's former husbands), was quite old when I met him at Frank's gallery. He was a fun and outgoing jet setter and invited me over to his studio in Sarasota. I was amazed at his imaginative paintings. His work was in the same vein as Salvador Dali. His exhibition was to follow Edna Hibel's. Edna often had sellouts and was considered the most successful female artist in the USA. I met Edna's mother, Lena, who was managing their Palm Beach gallery, a year before, but I never met Edna herself. Oehlaeger's had a good season for me and sold many of my paintings, as I broke into the Sarasota scene.

Several good seasons followed until I could see senility set in for Frank and he no longer recognized me. I became just another pedestrian to him. St. Armands' art scene disappeared because no gallery could afford the rising cost of real estate where only major clothing companies could make it. Frank died not too long after going out of business. One thing for sure—you can't rely on yesterday's successes.

Gordon Steele Memorial Award
12 x 12 in. | Oil on canvas | By Professor Hall Groat II

FAMILY TRIP TO SARASOTA

On a family trip to Sarasota one Easter we did the Sunday brunch at Jack's Marina. I had just delivered artwork to the gallery of Frank Oehlaeger on St. Armands Circle the day before. It was a perfect day, as the gulls swarmed over the bay. After brunch Captain Jack said the brunch and drinks were on the house. I thanked Jack, but was puzzled why he bought us this Easter dinner. He told me he and his son had just bought a new painting of mine at Oehlaeger's Gallery and that it brought them great joy this Easter.

I returned to Sarasota the following year to judge the Sarasota Art Association annual with a second juror, Valfred Thelin, a terrific watercolorist. I met Val at the Atlantic City Boardwalk Show a few years prior. I flew down and Val let me use his sleeping quarters and motorcycle to get to the beach. We went to a German beer hall in Bradenton and the next day went horseback riding at the art club director's ranch.

THE GINGERBREAD HOUSE

Henry Hudson Kitson, a noted sculptor, built his "Santarella"—a unique studio in historic Tyringham, Massachusetts, more commonly referred to as the "Gingerbread House." In his senior years he decided to call it a day and retire. Ann and Donald Davis were a young couple when they moved from New York City to the Berkshires. When they saw Kitson's gingerbread studio, they fell in love with it and decided to buy it and run it as an ice cream stand for the Berkshire tourists. Kitson's estate consisted of a large home with a pond on a gorgeous piece of property. The Gingerbread House was built for his working sculpture studio.

Donald spent his early years at General Electric, but when they decided to break into the gallery business full time, he took an early retirement from the Pittsfield, Massachusetts, company. In their early attempts to exhibit art, they landed Norman Rockwell, Harry Lane and other top artists. Donald wanted to handle more contemporary art and dropped Rockwell, which seemed illogical with such name recognition. Donald was a brilliant man, and well versed in art. His wife, Ann, loved by everyone, was a charming and gracious Italian woman who was kind and receptive to the customers. They raised two boys who helped in the gallery.

The sophisticated society painter Jan De Ruth summered at the Davis home for many years. Ann loved to entertain and the gallery had lavish dinner parties for artists and friends. They had masquerade parties and fund-raising events for the Shakespearean Theater. Jan and his family came out of a concentration camp via Ellis Island and made their mark in America. He became an important painter in New York and California and was often a guest on the *Johnny Carson*

Show. Jan used gorgeous young girls from a ballet school as models to paint. Ann Davis said she had to keep her eye on him when he took them up to the studio loft, as he was a smooth-talking ladies' man. His name had been assigned to him at Ellis Island when his whole family immigrated to America. Jan's sister was named Ruth so they assigned him to the name De Ruth. The family's name was Kleinholtz in Czechoslovakia. When he was a small boy, the Nazis spared his life so he could help cart bodies to the burial pits and crematoria. He was good at sketching, so the German officers traded him bread for his sketches. He showed me the numbers tattooed on his forearm. He told me his artwork saved his life as well as his sanity.

A few years after we met in Tyringham, Jan and I had a show together in Wilkes-Barre, Pennsylvania. He rode with me back to Manhattan, where there was a United Nations party being held in my honor. One of his comments to me on the trip was, "Hall, everything I look at looks like something you've painted." Annabelle Wiener, director at the World Federation of United Nations Associations (WFUNA), suggested I bring him along to a party at her East River penthouse. She kept an autograph book where artists and guests would sign in with funny jokes or sketches. Jan bluntly refused, saying, "All you want is a free drawing." Annabelle had a lavish catered party for ambassadors, a philatelic magazine publisher and Ole Hammond, chief of the U. N. Postal Administration. Because of his cavalier attitude, it was obvious Jan did not handle notoriety well. He was badly injured in a skiing accident the following winter in Colorado. A snow-grooming machine broke him up and he died a few years later. Ann was disgusted with Jan because he promised he was leaving her a painting in his will; however, it never materialized. The Davis family was very good to Jan when his father died. They allowed him to use their family plot in Tyringham Cemetery for burial, knowing New York City was very expensive.

Donald invited me in and handled my work for 45 years, until he died and Ann became too old to manage the business. My son, Hall II, also a painter, and my daughter, Gretchen, an outstanding mixed media collage artist, have had one-person shows there also. Donald was bipolar and artists often had a difficult time getting along with him. His wife spent much of her married life smoothing over artists and customers to avoid alienating them. She was a good person and he was, too, when you overlooked his mood swings.

Living in the Berkshire country had many advantages with Tanglewood's Music Center, Jacobs Pillow Dance Center, and the Berkshire Playhouse close at hand. Our family also took many enjoyable trips to Williamstown, visiting Clark Institute and Williams College, where I first exhibited in the Berkshires. My first major one-man show was at the Berkshire Museum in Pittsfield in 1962. The museum director, Stuart Henry, met with me after his daughter introduced us at a museum event. I won the Berkshire Art Association Purchase Prize for my painting *Megalopolis*. The judge was Lane Faison, director of Williams College Art School.

One summer weekend my wife, Rosemarie, and I were delivering new works to Tyringham, where a distinguished British doctor and his wife were in the process of buying one of my paintings. They introduced themselves, saying it was their second Groat work and they had bought one the year before. Dr. Thomson handed me his business card and he and his wife, Wendy, said if we ever visit the UK to please call them.

About a year later my wife and I decided on a trip to London. The Thomsons took a few days off, picked us up at our hotel, and took us to the prestigious Brooks's Club. In its 500-year history, no women were allowed. The club had just relaxed its rules and Rosemarie was one of the first American women admitted to have dinner there. Prince Charles and other royalty have membership at the club and many of the oldsters still mutter when a woman enters. When you arrive for cocktails, you're confronted by the paintings of Sir Henry Raeburn, R.A. (British, 1756-1823). While sitting at the massive table, you see the elaborate gold gilded centerpiece exactly as seen in his large painting. Most everything you see is older than America.

After drinks, we were taken into the dining room. Our hosts assumed we would not like the gamey taste of the British entrée, so the Thomsons ordered for us. After dinner we were escorted to the dessert room and then driven back to our hotel.

On our last night in London, Rosemarie and I walked aimlessly and came upon a lively party in a public building. It seemed interesting so we decided to crash it. A refined woman at a reception desk asked what we would like to drink and we said gin and tonic. She assumed we were just being funny with a weird American sense of humor; woops! We then saw a sign, "Alcoholics Anonymous."

The following summer we picked the Thomsons up in the Berkshires and gave them a tour around Greylock Mountain to Williams College, where some of his former classmates at Eton were on the faculty. I had made reservations for us all at a picturesque hotel outside of Williamstown. We had a champagne reception in a private room before entering the dining room. I mapped out a tour for them and the following morning they drove to Deerfield by way of the Mohawk Trail. We presented the British couple with a painting I had done for them, commemorating our first dinner at the Brooks's Club. It depicted the interior of the club, with an American and a British flag crossed. They later wrote us from London and said it was their favorite trip to the states. Being an artist offers extraordinary opportunities that otherwise may never have occurred, and you discover how small the world really is.

New York City Nocturne
41 x 22 in. | Oil on panel | By Hall Groat Sr.

THE PEN SKETCH

In 1993 I was called in to Chase Lincoln Bank to meet its vice president. He wanted a mural of Manlius that could be installed behind the teller's windows. He asked me if I had any ideas about cost and subject matter. We stepped over to an island used for customer transactions where I picked up a deposit slip, turned it over and drew a five-minute pen sketch. It suggested a scene of Manlius and surrounding landmarks with the swan pond in the foreground. I made notations of the proposed color scheme and then flipped the deposit slip over to the savings and withdrawal side and set the price. I was then asked about reproduction rights to print 200 serigraph prints, which doubled the price. We agreed on the proper size of the mural and the project was approved on-site.

In sales it is very important to have prompt answers so your customer doesn't have time to over-think the proposed project. It also shows the customer you know what you're talking about, which gives him confidence in you.

Arnie Poltensen, former owner of Salina Press, did a wonderful job on the edition of prints, and a media event was held in the bank for the unveiling of the mural. I autographed many prints for the bank's preferred customers. After ten years, the bank changed hands and the original mural was gifted to the Manlius Library and hung in the children's wing behind the checkout desk.

DARK HORSE CREEK GALLERY

After having one-man shows around the country, I found one of the best openings of my career was in Erieville—a small town in Central New York, where I maintained a studio for two years. Tim Tormey was the director of the Dark Horse Creek Gallery and his attention to detail was extraordinary. Some art openings are dry, but Tim created a party atmosphere that made being an artist a pleasure. It was a retrospective of my work that spanned sixty years.

NEW BRUNSWICK SAVINGS BANK

In the 1970s Mr. Bier, president of New Brunswick Savings Bank, was very anxious for me to visit his Highland branch bank to discuss a mural project. It was short notice and I brought my portfolio of other bank murals to give him ideas to consider. As I drove down the Garden State Parkway and arrived at my exit, I took a break to gather my thoughts and impressions of the New Brunswick area. Sitting in a diner with a coffee, I picked up a napkin and sketched my impression of the area with its many bridges and the industrial view east of the parkway toward the Atlantic. It was all very new to me, but I felt it was important to have some understanding of the area. When I met Mr. Bier he seemed more interested in my little napkin sketch than the photos of other projects in my portfolio. Somehow I had captured the essence of the city and the finished mural never deviated much from my napkin sketch. And like all bankers, his first question was, "How much?" I was a little on the low side, as I didn't see him as a big spender and I didn't want to gamble on losing this job. Instead, I requested my full travel expenses and accommodations. The deal was made in about 15 minutes and we shook hands. The project was fun and all the employees just stared in awe at this young brush slinger up on the wall. Mr. Bier never came by to see my work until an incident was brought to his attention. In my second week of work, a group of black people came in to request that I change some of my figures to represent their race. I explained to them that I was under contract to the bank and they should ask the bank president. Mr. Bier finally came by to request that no changes be made and I never saw him again. The bankers were very friendly and invited me out for drinks on a few occasions. Many years later I was taking my son to a tennis tournament close to New Brunswick and he wanted to see the mural. When we walked into the bank building the interior was completely changed and a new business was there. The wall that was once my mural was covered over with mirrors. All I have to show is my scale model that hangs in my studio and a napkin sketch.

CHAPTER 4

DARK SIDE OF MY CAREER

GALLERY AT HOP MEADOW

Although most Central New York art galleries are reputable, it's important to expand your horizon to other states. Simsbury, a bedroom community of Hartford, Connecticut, had the Hop Meadow gallery. Arlene, the director, was good at marketing and a masterful salesperson, and I had some great years dealing with her. During the tech boom she was aggressive about getting her artists in the major corporations and banks in and around Hartford. Her gallery was leading the way in sales at that time. She moved east after her job at Braniff airlines ended when the company went into bankruptcy. We all know what happened when the bubble burst—companies downsized and too often failed to pay their bills. Like a house of cards, the major customers faced cash flow problems and bankruptcy. The artists lost their work, the money owed to them evaporated and the art world died. It was every man for himself, and you had to hound the gallery for monies due from art sales.

Franklin Jones was the best-selling artist in the gallery. His work was of the Americana genre and loved by the more conservative collectors. I called him at his Stockbridge studio and asked him if he had received any checks from the gallery. He chastised me for questioning the director's integrity. He was owed eighty-five thousand dollars, and she informed him he should not worry, as the companies were a little slow with their payments. I wished him luck, but knew we were all being scammed. I called her every single morning for two months. Finally, I got most of the money due to me; however, Franklin surprised me with his naiveté. He got bilked. According to my friend, watercolorist Robert Daley of Holyoke, Massachusetts, Franklin was last seen sitting on a curbstone in Pittsfield, looking dejected. He tried to sue the gallery owner, but she had no remaining assets. Soon after, he had a stroke and lost most of his eyesight.

At an earlier time, Franklin had teamed up with Norman Rockwell to create the now defunct Famous Artists School in Westport, Connecticut. They both lost their shirts. Norman alone lost a million dollars on that investment. Overall, in ten years with the gallery, I did well. The director died rather young along with the hopes and dreams of scores of her stable of artists.

WILKES-BARRE FLOOD

I was exhibiting at a gallery in Wilkes-Barre, Pennsylvania, where my major paintings were displayed in the front windows. Several weeks after the opening, a catastrophic flood swept through the city. I lost all my art and was never remunerated. A year later a family who had recovered one of my paintings from the flood contacted me. It was easy to restore. Basically, I removed the gray silt in stages and found no damage other than slight warping. Thousands of people had to evacuate their homes as the water level rose to the rooflines. A family I knew had a pet canary and they hung it in its cage from their attic ceiling before they ran for their lives. When the waters finally receded, a water level mark could be seen just below the bird's swing. It lived to sing another day. As for my years' work in art, some pictures may be dug up in reconstruction efforts in Wilkes-Barre. The creative effort, in itself, was probably more beneficial to me than the monetary value. I considered it a minor setback in my long art career.

Provincetown Library
24 x 18 in. | Oil on canvas | By Hall Groat Sr.

THE ALBANY LOBBYISTS

About fifteen years ago I had a call from Roy, a former customer of mine. He may have meant well, but what he suggested became a nightmare for me. Some Albany lobbyists wanted a large group of paintings to fill their offices for a party. They informed me they would choose which ones they wanted to buy from the selection presented. They sounded serious enough so I gave it my immediate attention. It was a rush deal because I had to deliver on the following morning.

I enlisted the help of my son, who was my right-hand man. We had to check over all the art and upgrade the framing so as to be ready for hanging. I had to prepare the list of sizes and prices and then load the work into my vehicle. We had to leave at five a.m. because we had to hang the paintings in all of their offices. I'm sure they were pleased with the way their place looked for the big party, but I was insulted when I wasn't invited.

When my son and I were returning home, I began to get that sinking feeling. Sure enough, that premonition I had was correct. I had just been conned by an arrogant group of lobbyists. When I asked if they had made any decisions on which art they were going to buy, they informed me a few politicians were interested in them. They gave me a name of one of those so-called "interested parties," but when I called him he didn't know anything about it. It was a cruel hoax. I approached the lobbyists about paying some of my delivery expenses, but they were rude and unreceptive to this reasonable suggestion. They told me they were *doing me a favor* to let me hang my work in their offices—that it was good exposure. In business you meet all kinds, but these scoundrels are without conscience and well insulated with giant egos. Lobbyists! They will go down as the worst people I have ever dealt with.

GALLERY THEFT IN THE 1980s

The Little Gallery on Broad Street in Philadelphia handled my work for about seven years. When the gallery hired a new director, he wanted only the New York City avant-garde work and asked all artists to pick up their paintings. When I arrived on a Saturday, several works were missing and the gallery assumed no responsibility. They instead offered me other artists' work that had been discarded, to help cover the loss. All the other unframed art had been left behind by out-of-town artists who simply decided to leave it with the gallery. This is an example of what goes on and how artists can be cheated when work is on consignment.

A TIME TO GIVE UP ON THE MARINE PAINTING

Sometimes in your art career you accept a commission you're not at home with. A woman commissioned a portrait of her husband whom she wanted to surprise with a small portrait. I soon found many factors involved with the job became insurmountable. The reference photos were not adequate and conclusive; therefore, I just could not get a handle on it. She supplied me with a high school photo and another of him when he was in the service. The service photo showed two soldiers and her husband's head was leaning to one side as if he was talking to his friend.

She asked me to straighten out his head and put a marine dress hat and jacket on him. My first gut feeling was to not take this commission, but the lady was anxious for me to try. After doing it over many times and failing miserably, I should have given up. With a poor reference photo and trying to put a hat and jacket on him from photos found on a Google search, there was no way to achieve a likeness. If the customer had supplied a photo with her husband wearing the proper attire, it may have been possible. The fact is everyone looks different with a hat on and I was playing a guessing game. I had no idea when I had achieved a likeness. I was going in circles and was very frustrated. It's not in my personality to give up, but this time I had no choice.

AVOIDING ARREST IN BAR HARBOR

After I finished a mural for the Merrill Trust Company in Bangor, Maine, our family drove east to Bar Harbor. I found it so picturesque I decided to paint a few color studies in the town park. While I was painting, with my wife and two kids with me, a man approached me about buying one of the small, unframed works. I told him I was not there to sell art. He told me he was visiting and wanted to bring a gift to his son. He was mature and dressed in construction clothes and work boots. He had cold blue eyes and was Germanic looking. I didn't think of him as the type who would be buying art. I was about ready to pack up and take my family to the beach, but he kept pressing me to buy an unframed small painting. I agreed and as he handed me the money, a police officer jumped from a bush behind me and the two men began to make an arrest. I said, "Wait! I never attempted to sell you anything. You were the one pressing to buy. Also, these are just little doodles of no particular value." He said, "OK then, the next passerby will get one of your paintings." A young couple came by pushing a baby carriage. They accepted the painting, but looked very puzzled. I let him play his little game to avoid being arrested for "selling without a license." If I didn't, we could have been held up for days at great expense so it was well worth the little doodle. Before leaving Bar Harbor, I asked the young policeman who this man was. He informed me the man was the retired chief of police in Bar Harbor and owner of Webber Construction Company. When we checked out of our motel three days early, I told the proprietor she could blame Webber, the chief of police, for her business loss. Entrapment is against the law.

NEW ART GALLERY: A DUBIOUS VENTURE

Two middle-aged men from Connecticut started a gallery business on Route No. 7, the main drag in Pittsfield, Massachusetts. It became apparent to me they knew little about art when I stopped by one day. They had expressed an interest in making money and setting up a little school in their basement. When I later went to observe their students at work, several women were at their easels painting a figure duet from life. The subject consisted of two nude models entwined in an erotic entanglement. A white woman and a black man were posed on a raised platform with dim, tinted lights that showed the contours of their naked figures. As I observed the artists' progress, the male became noticeably aroused and there was a tense moment on the modeling platform. The woman pulled away and the male went after her in a chase. An artist ran to the model's rescue by giving the male model a few good whacks across his back with her long-handled paintbrush, subduing him. The young black model had paint splattered all over his backside and looked frightened and embarrassed. He left the gallery quickly, ending his brief career as a nude model. The gallery owners secretly filmed the whole episode. They were using the gallery as a front for their gambling and porn operation. Many artists discovered their work had been stolen, as the business was shut down and the two owners received jail sentences.

Stuart Henry, Berkshire Museum director, expressed his displeasure with local artists who displayed their work in this "dubious gallery." Their lack of judgment created a black eye for an art community committed to establishing a wholesome atmosphere for the people of Pittsfield. However, many new galleries and cultural institutions have since been created.

PURCHASE AWARD FOR A FORGERY

In the late 1960s I stopped by the Berkshire Museum in Pittsfield. The Art Association Annual Exhibition was installed and it is always a good show. As I walked around the room, I saw the works of many Berkshire friends. Since I had moved back to Syracuse, I had not entered any of my works in years. It came as a complete shock to see one of my paintings with a savings bank purchase award on it. My signature had been rubbed out and another man had signed it. I went to the museum office and reported this person, whom I happened to know. The museum just hushed it up and offered no apology to me. It was pathetic of this amateur artist to stoop so low as to enter my work as his own. I felt pity on him. I sent him a letter of congratulations for his cash award and suggested he should enter his own painting in the future. He sent me a plaque he had made up with a biography of my career etched in gold. I suppose he felt this would compensate for his forgery. But he stopped short of admitting his crime. I could have listed this award he won on my resume, but I was beyond a point in my career that it had much relevance. It shows how desperate some wannabe artists are for recognition.

Brooklyn Bridge
33 x 12 in. | Oil on canvas | By Hall Groat Sr.

THE UNTRUSTWORTHY:
THE SALE THAT GOT AWAY

One summer in Pittsfield, I was showing work for sale on the museum lawn along with the art league. I was twenty-nine years old and my car had just blown an engine, so making money was important. It was a windy day and difficult to keep the display of paintings standing. There was a crowd around my art, when a gust of wind blew some paintings at the customers. I quickly blurted out, "If you caught it, you bought it."

This was so entertaining an event that people started buying some of the works. A couple from New Jersey told me they wanted to buy my larger work priced at $400. I agreed and assumed it was sold. Within a few seconds a young couple on their honeymoon came running up to me wagging four 100-dollar bills. They said they had decided to forego their honeymoon for the purchase of my painting. I informed them another couple had spoken first. The young couple left—a little too quickly—because the first couple started hedging, asked to have the painting held up again, and then changed their minds. I needed that sale at that particular time very badly. I lost the sale by respecting the verbal commitment of this first couple. For years I have asked businesspeople how they would have handled it. Some said they would have honored the verbal commitment of the first couple, while others say they would not have. To coin an old cliché, "Money talks louder than words." I was a naïve and a trusting fool. I should have grabbed the cash.

I'D GIVE MY RIGHT ARM FOR A MILLION DOLLARS

Living in a rooming house in my late twenties was rather bleak. A few dropouts and a filthy bathroom to share down the hall were a short-lived experience. I coped with it for a while as I awaited an opening in an apartment complex. My room was a block from Westcott Street in Syracuse, where there was a breakfast nook, Pop Welch's bar, and Frank's Pizza across from the "Wescot," a movie house. Neighborhoods are fun, providing you move away before you become too engrained in the lifestyle.

One of the roomers stood outside my open door. He often stopped and passed a few words from the hallway. He was a friendly guy, but seemed depressed. The last time we spoke he confided in me that he was broke and felt out of place at his workplace. He was from New England and a dysfunctional home. He said his family was disappointed he was a factory worker and they expected more from him. As his eyes scanned the walls, I could tell he enjoyed taking in the paintings that I rotated periodically. He asked what it was like being an artist and wished he had a decent career other than his dismal hourly job. What he was about to say next should have tipped me off that he had a self-destructive personality. I should have considered his remark a foreshadowing of what was to occur in a few days. "I'd give my right arm for a million dollars." His remark led me to ask, "If you could buy anything in the world you want with that million, what would it be?" He paused and answered, "My arm back." We smiled at his dark humor, but a few days later the landlady informed me he had gone home—crawled under his running car, wrapped his head up into the tailpipe and committed suicide.

Looking back, I wished I had invited him into my room so we could have talked more about art. Who knows, that might have given him something positive to think about and offered me the opportunity to show him, through an artist's eyes, that things aren't as bad as they seem.

THE IMPORTANCE OF GOOD COMMUNICATION

When you're dealing with second-hand information, a commission job can turn into disaster. Such was my misfortune that summer on Cape Cod in 1972. Thomas Gaglione ran a great gallery in Wellfleet and one of his customers wanted him to have an artist do a painting of her bayside cottage. Tom called me and asked if I would do the job. It sounded easy and when I finished it, I delivered it to the gallery for the customer to come in and have a look. The woman told Tom it was wrong because she had ordered a painting depicting a scene looking out to the water from inside the cottage. I had wasted my time and was not about to do it over. These things happen when you go through a middle person. It was very strange and annoying to me and I always thought she may have changed her mind and just used that as a ploy. What do you think?

Museum School, Clark Institute
24 x 24 in. | Oil on panel | By Hall Groat Sr.

PATTY TERRY GALLERY: ABSENTEE LANDLORD

The first gallery I showed with on St. Armands Circle, Sarasota, was run by a fine woman, who took care of business in a responsible way. Patty, along with husband Terry, always represented my work in a professional manner. There were many sales made for me, although I still maintained my own business in upstate New York. Carlton was a retired interior designer from New England who worked with the gallery. When our family arrived in Sarasota for the first time, Carlton drove us everywhere to familiarize us with the area. This was especially important for me, as I needed to photograph subject matter in preparation for new paintings of Florida. For a period of time, Carlton ran the business while the Terry family was away.

Carlton was living with a new wife at their Bird Isle Glass home. Carlton's marital relationship became compromised when his interest swayed to a young man who helped out at the gallery. I had never met this young man, although had no reason for concern at the time. Carlton put too much trust in his new partner, and paintings began to disappear. During Carlton's periodic business travels, his companion ran the gallery alone. It was brought to my attention that my large vertical painting entitled *Nassah Window*, which was featured on the exhibition program cover, had been stolen, as well as a few other works. This marked the end of my relationship with this gallery. It had seen better days and the business dissolved. This loss represented a substantial amount of money to me and any attempts made to recover my loss proved futile.

TOO GOOD TO BE TRUE

When I was living in Cazenovia in my mid-thirties, two gentlemen who owned a gallery in Kalamazoo, Michigan, stopped by to see my artwork. After looking through my paintings, these smooth-talking men decided they wanted to handle my work on a continual basis, because I had the look they were positive was right for their gallery. They agreed to pay me $50,000 per year if I would ship them my entire output of art. Sounded like a good opportunity so I went along with the deal. In a few weeks, I shipped them a box of art and ten days later my first check arrived. Several weeks later, I shipped them my second box of art, but this time there was no response and no check. Their first payment was to establish their credibility, and then they just stole the next shipment. They were con artists and I got ripped off. Many years later, I had a call from a party in Kalamazoo who asked for an appraisal of their painting. When I asked the name of the gallery they bought it from, it was a match: Four Winds Gallery, Kalamazoo. I informed the folks requesting the appraisal that their painting was stolen and I refused to appraise it.

CHAPTER 5

SPECIAL COMMISSIONS

WORLD FEDERATION OF UNITED NATIONS ASSOCIATIONS

In 1969 I received a call from the executive director of the World Federation of United Nations Associations (WFUNA) with an urgent request. Annabelle Wiener was a friend I met while summering in Manhasset, Long Island, as a teenager. She and husband Bob were friends of my sister, Priscilla, who was their neighbor. Artist Ben Shahn was scheduled to have his first-day-of- issue cover design (envelope) ready for publication, but had died suddenly. I had a reputation as a reliable artist who could deliver on schedule. She had two days before going to press and one day for me to come up with my design for the Labor and Development program.

After burning the midnight oil, I came up with a first day cover (FDC) that was well received by the chief of the U.N. Postal Administration. I was invited to fly to New York City for an unveiling party at a luncheon in U.N. headquarters. The rest of the afternoon was spent meeting stamp collectors from every corner of the globe and autographing the first day covers. I continued this volunteer activity for the next 12 years. Of my ten designs for WFUNA, my Picasso FDC drew the longest lines of collectors.

At the end of the workday I was often taken to a restaurant, following cocktails in the ambassador's lounge. I often stayed at the United Nations Ambassador Hotel. On the night of my last trip the director took me out to a famous French restaurant. After dinner, they had the waiters remove the tablecloth and circle our table as we unwound by shooting craps until midnight. Annabelle said it was getting late so we rolled the dice for the pot. I won!

Rosemarie Groat, Hall Groat Sr. and Priscilla Grauer (sister)
at United Nations ambassador's party in New York City.

FIRST DAY COVERS
FOR ART LOVERS AND PHILATELISTS ALIKE

In its 1972 winter issue, Northeast Airlines' *In-flight Magazine* published a two-page spread covering the first day covers that had been produced by WFUNA. Distinguished artists, such as Salvador Dali, Marc Chagall, Pablo Picasso and William Gropper, were featured. The article highlighted ten first day covers—including two of mine. I was honored to be recognized with these great artists in this issue. My first design published represented Labor and Development, a 1969 issue. My most notable work was issued in 1971. It was to commemorate Picasso's ninetieth birthday. Pablo Picasso personally approved my work, which had to complement the portrait of his daughter Maya. This issue broke all records in sales for WFUNA. All the artwork is included in the United Nations Philatelic Museum at Palais des Nations in Geneva, Switzerland.

ST. JAMES CHURCH

A friend and old customer suggested I contact the Rev. John Finnegan, pastor of the St. James Church in Syracuse. He had a vision of a mural he wanted me to paint behind the altar. We agreed on the fee and he approved my scale model. A contractor erected scaffolding, and I was under way. Somehow the wheels were not attached correctly and the scaffolding tipped forward and then backward in a sudden lurch. My buckets of oil color went splashing across the white marble altar. Father Finnegan came out of his office with an armful of towels and together we cleaned it up. He was very understanding and realized the accident was not my fault. The church organist often practiced as I worked on the mural and realized the music served as inspiration while I painted. My son, Hall II, helped with preliminary measurements and layout. He was experienced and had worked with me on many projects. I also donated a series of paintings that gave a feeling of continuity within the church.

ST. ELIZABETH ANN SETON

When Father Finnegan was assigned as pastor of the contemporary church St. Elizabeth Ann Seton in Baldwinsville, New York, he asked me to design another mural. The church was actually designed by his brother, Maurice. I designed this work to complement the building, yet maintain the peaceful and spiritual environment. It was monochromatic and quiet. Many parishioners have commented to me on the beautiful feeling the mural gives them—and that's exactly what I intended to achieve. The church has many of my paintings in other classrooms and office areas. Monsignor Joseph Champlain donated the mural.

ST. JOHN THE EVANGELIST

During an outdoor exhibit to benefit the Canal Museum in downtown Syracuse, I met the pastor of St. John the Evangelist Church, Father Thomas Fitzpatrick. He and Sister Judy invited me to walk over to their church and asked for my thoughts on the vestibule. It was very large, but devoid of visual interest. We all agreed that facing murals on each side of the vestibule would give a warm feeling when parishioners entered the church. I showed my scale models with the proposal and the project was accepted. They allowed me to use the belfry tower as a temporary studio. It worked out well and I felt as though I had stepped back into an earlier age in history. My son again assisted me as I stretched the linen canvas out on the 11-foot wooden bars. When the murals were finished and approved, we slid them over the choir loft to the outstretched hands of a paperhanger, who removed them from their stretchers and permanently glued them to the walls. An expert woodworker built two wooden frames and a protective wooden rail. Many parishioners expressed their joy in seeing the history of their church in these murals.

Hall Groat in belfry tower with murals in progress at
St. John the Evangelist Church, Syracuse, New York.

PYRAMID COMPANIES

Bob and Susan Congel enjoyed playing tennis at Limestone Tennis Club. It was also the club our family and many neighbors frequented. Bob, who heads the Pyramid Companies, often had to cancel because like any great businessman, it's work before play. I became his frequent substitute and enjoyed his group of friends: Fran Lombardi, Pat Bright, John Murphy and others. One day after Bob and I teamed up as doubles partners, he asked me to bring a painting he admired in the club's social lounge to his office at Widewaters, DeWitt. It was just the beginning. He bought art for all of his homes, offices and his Stratton Mt. ski lodge.

NORTH MEDICAL CENTER

During the 1990s I was doing proposal work for the North Medical Center in Liverpool, New York. My first assignment was an office mural depicting the many activities in the medical profession. It made an interesting picture in the waiting room. My next project was to design a large sign for the top of the medical center. It later developed into a logo design and was used for all advertising and promotional signs.

A few years later I painted a mural in the Atrium Café at North Medical Center that added visual interest for patients and medical staff.

New York Stock Exchange
40 x 30 in. | Oil on canvas | By Hall Groat Sr.

CANAL MURAL IN CANASTOTA

Dick Clark of Cazenovia has been a customer of mine for many years. He owns Clark Gas Company and the Nice N Easy store in Canastota and was instrumental in the early development of these stores. John MacDougall, who also owns several of the stores, invited me to submit a proposal for an outside mural that would highlight the history of the Erie Canal. Canastota was a stop for canal travel and commerce. Although I had never considered doing outdoor murals, I thought it would be fun to work on location. This mural was a competition and my competitor had done numerous exterior wall murals in Syracuse and Central New York and was very experienced. My scale model was for a 30-foot-wide scene of the mules, led by farmers pulling the canal boats along the towpath. I used a very bold design that would catch the eyes of people driving by on Route 5, Canastota. The Nice N Easy store's owner and the employees used a democratic way of deciding the winner, and I won by one vote.

The painting was laid out on heavy 4-by-8-foot plywood panels lined up across my garage floor. When I had the basic idea down, I leaned them against a hedgerow of arborvitae so I could better visualize the complete canal scene. I used the brightest and boldest colors available because sunlight always fades colors and I wanted to maximize the life of this mural. A construction crew mounted the panels in a large frame. At that point, I had to work on ladders to carry it to completion, which took about a month. Approximately ten years later I repainted the whole mural exactly the same as originally seen with the help of artist friend Wayne Daniels. It's a great conversation piece for tourists who frequent this Nice N Easy store. Many travelers and locals stopped by to watch my progress. One couple from New England later sent me a warm letter with photos of the work in progress.

PAINTING FOR ENTRANCE OF LORETTO CHAPEL

In 2008 I was commissioned by Robert and Frances Byrne to prepare a series of studies in acrylic. One of these studies would eventually be selected by the Byrnes and a committee to be the subject of a large oil painting planned to be hung outside the chapel on the main floor of the new Loretto Chapel. The subject consisted of an elderly couple being received by Christ, with the white dove overhead representing the Holy Spirit. The simplicity of the subject made every detail and gesture of the three figures extremely difficult. The slightest adjustment in a hand or angle of a head was critical and could give the work an entirely different feeling. The painting falls loosely into the category of surrealism, although not in a classic sense. The two figures in the foreground were painted in a representational way, but the total work takes on a personal meaning depending on the viewer's interpretation. This 48-by-72-inch oil painting was dedicated as a permanent religious icon and has been viewed by thousands of residents and guests of Loretto.

JOHN MULROY TRIBUTE

When John Mulroy, our longtime county executive, retired, I was honored with the commission of painting a story of his many accomplishments. It took research and time to gather all the information I needed. My nephew John Groat was instrumental in securing the reference material that made the painting special. The original art was 30 by 40 inches and is now owned by the Mulroy family. Due to the community's interest in this painting, an edition of serigraph prints was produced and the prints are in the collections of many of Mulroy's fans throughout Central New York as well as in governmental offices. A large portrait of our former county executive is permanently hung in the John Mulroy Civic Center.

WORLD WAR II FIGHTER PLANE

Dr. Robert Cady contacted me years back about creating a painting of his father's Curtis P-40 WWII fighter plane. He brought a good photo reference to my studio that indicated every detail that made his aircraft unique. I had painted many fighter planes, including a B-29 for a neighbor who also enjoyed building models of fighter planes. In talking with Bob, I mentioned my father had a good friend who would stop by the house when I was a boy. My mother used to complain because he always smelled the house up with his strong cigars. His name was Al Cady and he owned the Rome Soap Company. "Any relation?" I asked. Bob said, "Oh, yeah, he was my grandfather." That brought back memories for us both.

PATRICK BARRETT MONTAGE PAINTING

Christine Barrett contacted me about doing a montage painting as a tribute to her husband, Patrick, for Christmas several years ago. She was well prepared with photos of his boyhood home and large family, along with the family car. She even supplied me with his Siena College crest to be incorporated into the painting, as well as his favorite haunt in New York City. This was the largest work of its kind for a private citizen I have done to date. It's certainly the ultimate tribute and was unveiled in his living room Christmas morning.

FIFTIETH ANNIVERSARY SURPRISE

When Mel Rubenstein contacted me a few years ago about doing a painting honoring his wife, Mady, on their 50th anniversary, we talked a while about growing up on the eastside of Syracuse. We discovered we had played against each other in sandlot football next to Meadowbrook Parkway when we were about twelve. I remembered as a kid going to the business his family owned, Rochester Sample Shoe Store, where my mother took me to get ready for school. It's good to know a little about a customer and helps to develop a good working relationship. We soon talked about where the painting would hang and other details about the color and size of this commission. Our second meeting was at his home, where he showed me his art collection and then took me to the dining room, where he had spread out hundreds of photos of Mady and extended family. Vacations in Europe, ski trips and parties, along with Mady's fabulous kitchen with a brick oven, helped to make the painting unique. Mel had done a fabulous job gathering exactly the right reference material, including pictures of the family pets, for me. I selected the photos I knew would be conducive to creating a great painting. I took them to my studio where I laid them out on a large piece of brown paper that was cut to the proper size we had planned. With my rough color sketches on the paper, Mel was able to visualize my layout for the painting. Many months later, when the final painting on canvas was finished and framed, it was hung over the mantel. It made a great surprise for Mady and the whole family.

NEIGHBOR COMMISSIONED A PIRATE SHIP

People never cease to amaze me. Several summers ago I received a painting commission that was to be hung in Bill and Beverly Egan's new home in North Carolina. After doing several thousand paintings, this was the most unusual request I have ever dealt with. The painting was a foreshadowing of what to expect from pirates in the Gulf of Aden and Indian Ocean. The Egans must have had psychic powers, because I no sooner finished the painting than the pirates attacked our shipping lanes.

As I worked on this large oil, my mind was on "Old Blackbeard" and how he looked standing near the bow of my pirate ship. I was depicting a scene in history, but never dreamed modern day pirates would reappear to rob and pillage our citizens. History really does repeat itself and the Egans must have been aware of this possibility. Was this a strange coincidence, or did Bill and Beverly know something about "Old Blackbeard" that I missed?

CHAPTER 6

RECOGNITION AND AWARDS

FIRST AWARD

The most important art award I have ever won may surprise the reader. It was the high school scholastic gold key I won while a student at Nottingham. That inspired me to pursue art as a career. Many kids have won several gold keys, portfolio awards, and have received high grades on their work in school. I only had one, but often wonder what I would have done had I not received my lone gold key for a watercolor. Perhaps I would have chosen a different direction in life. Without doubt, that scholastic gold key ranks at the top of my award list.

WCNY PUBLIC TELEVISION

Dick Russell, president of WCNY TV, called me to be the first artist in Central New York to be the subject of a documentary. When the camera crew and producer arrived at my home/ studio we first did a personal interview, then they filmed the studio, Rosemarie's gardens, the family, and my personal collections. I decided my customers would do a better job talking about their "Groat" collections than I would, so I handed them a list of names and addresses of the companies that were my major collectors. It was a good decision on my part and a way of honoring corporations that had been loyal to me, as well as highlighting their workplaces. It was interesting to hear the way each CEO discussed the art, what it meant to the employees, how it made for a warmer working environment, the financial arrangement we had, and why they enjoyed doing business with me.

Some of the company heads were liberal arts educated and very astute about the arts. They would discuss each of my works as if it were a museum tour. Others admitted they didn't know much about art, but spoke from the heart and in their own way were able to say what they liked about a given painting. These executives made the documentary more interesting than any one artist could do simply because they spoke candidly and did not use a script. *Hall Groat: A Man and His Art* was not only aired by WCNY, but also requested by many art groups to show at their meetings.

Art critic Clement Greenberg attended the WCNY reception for Tel-Auc. My work was being featured at the Everson Museum, as I had donated many pieces to the fund-raiser and the documentary film was about to be aired. He was very complimentary about my paintings and told me I was "an artist who could make it." I thanked him and asked if he would put it in writing. He wrote it out for me, then and there, and signed his name.

Hall Groat: A Man and His Art
WCNY Public Television Documentary

ASSOCIATED ARTISTS OF SYRACUSE

Syracuse was holding a competition at the Syracuse Museum of Fine Arts—forerunner of the Everson Museum of Art. At the urging of artist Gordon Steele, I joined the Associated Artists, a group of local artists. The first event they had was a sketch show. My mother joined me while I went out sketching. We ended up at the Onondaga reservation. There I spotted a dilapidated barn for a subject. I was less than impressed with my results, so before we left the reservation I tossed the sketch into a trash barrel. My mother emphatically said, "No! Your sketch is too good to throw away." I retrieved it and entered it in the show. The three judges picked it as the "best in show." That was a very meaningful award, because to win among professional artists is important if you expect to go anywhere. Years later I was awarded two Gordon Steele Memorial Medals. Thanks, Mom!

THE BERKSHIRE MUSEUM

In 1962 I won the Berkshire Museum top prize, the BAA, in Pittsfield, Massachusetts, for my six-foot *Megalopolis*. It also was a museum purchase award that was followed by an invitation for a one-man show. When the museum hung it in its permanent collection, it was next to Norman Rockwell's *Barbershop Quartet*. Rockwell expressed a strong interest in my work and, along with museum director Stuart Henry, made plans to take me to lunch. Rockwell often complained he was thought of as just an illustrator and wanted to be accepted as a painter. He proved to the world he is an important artist and the distinction between illustrator and painter has since faded away. The people have spoken louder than the critics on his behalf.

Barbershop Quartet by Norman Rockwell
Megalopolis by Hall Groat Sr.
1962 Berkshire Museum Purchase Prize and Groat at age 29

MUSEUM COLLECTION

There is no reason to belabor the subject of awards, as the list would soon be forgotten. After all, "success is not an art contest," but it's important to be part of a museum collection, and purchase prizes are often a way to achieve that goal. Several years ago I was in the Albright Knox western regional show in Buffalo with my contemporary portrait of Ernest Hemingway. There were very few painters accepted in this show, so I considered that an honor. The greater the collection one is part of, the more an artist becomes part of history. Many estates bequeath artworks to museums for tax planning. But after the works are amassed in museum storage racks, they are often auctioned or sold off in years to come. Acceptance in national shows is prestigious to an emerging artist, but not always a precursor of success. When I was starting out, many artists wanted to be in the Rockefeller collection. Being in the IBM collection is another nice addition to a resume. In the final analysis, if an artist's work is truly great, it will surface at some point in time.

ARTHUR FIEDLER

When the Syracuse Symphony Orchestra (SSO) invited Arthur Fiedler to conduct about 30 years ago, the atmosphere was exciting at Fayetteville High School. He was being honored there the night before his SSO concert. The following day, I was a member of a small party at his luncheon table at the Onondaga Country Club. One thing that became apparent to me was Fiedler enjoyed talking about cooking and collecting cooking utensils rather than music. But he soon switched the conversation to his interest in fire trucks, which were his lifetime hobby, and fires. As a fire buff, he was often seen chasing fires in Boston. I can appreciate that because talking about your profession on your day off at a luncheon can be monotonous. He was a fun-loving person who everyone enjoyed being with. I designed the SSO program cover with my impression of Fiedler. The Dwyers of Cazenovia own the original art.

LEOPOLD STOKOWSKI AT REHEARSAL

During a rehearsal about 25 years ago in a school auditorium, I was doing some watercolor studies of Leopold Stokowski, the great conductor. He was rehearsing with the Syracuse Symphony Orchestra for an upcoming concert. He became irate at the orchestra, put on his coat and headed for the door. Stokowski claimed the librarian handed out the wrong music. But it was only dramatics, as he soon returned and continued conducting. Later in the evening he called me to the podium to see my artwork. He made a negative gesture with his nose, so I asked what he found so offensive. He told me his former wife was a great artist, and he knew good art when he saw it. I said, "Maestro, Gloria Vanderbilt was not a great artist—she was a designer." The conversation ended there, but the music was sensational.

Maestro Leopold Stokowski summons Hall Groat Sr. to the podium.

WASHINGTON AND JEFFERSON TWO-MAN SHOW

My son and I were invited to exhibit our work at the art school at Washington and Jefferson College, in Washington, Pennsylvania. The director of the fine arts department failed to have his students present at the opening. It was a Friday night and he would have had to make attendance mandatory. College students usually hit the pubs or fraternity parties and often forget why they're in college.

When we arrived at the beautifully installed exhibition, only the art director was there. After driving from Manlius, New York, to Pennsylvania, it was a big let-down. I decided to take it upon myself to salvage this opening. I walked through the art building and solicited students to come to the exhibit and hear a wonderful art lecture by my son. A small group of students arrived and was truly interested in learning and discussing the exhibit. Sometimes in life when people don't do their job, you must take the "bull by the horns." It turned out to be a memorable event.

CHAPTER 7

VIEWPOINTS ON ART

COMPOSITION

Many students are born with a natural sense of composition and for those who are not endowed with this natural ability, I share your scorn. It seems unfair some students have a natural ability to compose a picture, while others have not the foggiest notion of where to start. Hereditary factors beyond our control often leave us inept when it comes to composing a picture. Why would anyone want to enter the art field with this deficiency? It seems rather masochistic to attempt working on art when you have no idea what the hell you're doing. The student next to you in kindergarten comes up with a great design and you come up empty handed, hoping the teacher will show you some way to create a presentable crayon drawing. You may even be passed over when the teacher allows students to paint at the easel. After all, you only know how to scribble and many other kids already do stick figures with a big sunshine placed perfectly in the right upper portion of their composition.

My younger brother Roderic must have shared the same feelings in elementary school. When the teacher asked the class to draw a picture of a bird, he gave it his best shot. However, he drew his bird with four legs. On parent-teacher night, the teacher told our mother that when she asked Roddy why he drew four legs under his bird, he answered, "So it wouldn't tip over." Although atypical, his answer seems logical. However, great modern artists conjure up much wackier creations than Roddy's bird. Marc Chagall and Pablo Picasso come to mind when I think of taking such liberties in art.

The compulsion to paint may be a greater force than your inability in composition so there is no reason not to charge ahead. After all, not everyone need be the best, although you may still be a player.

EDUCATION

Now that you have established the fact that you may not stack up in comparison to your classmates, you may find yourself in a unique position. Your artwork may be passed over and the teacher may leave you out when she pins up those student drawings with stickers of excellence in the corner. Because you fail to impress anyone, nothing is expected of you and the teacher will invariably devote more attention to the talented ones destined for greatness. This is where you make your move! Think of yourself as a track star pacing behind the pack, only to blow past your opponents at the finish line. The resources are available and you must self-educate. To put your life in the hands of a teacher, who may be overloaded with classroom work and fails to see your talent, may be a mistake. Get yourself a library card. Go to the art section and start looking at pictures. When you see a painting you love, study everything about it. Ask yourself why you like it, and how the artist composed it. Close the book and close your eyes. Try to remember everything you can about this painting. Take a sheet of computer paper and try to diagram what you remember. First in simple lines, then with tones using the side of a soft lead pencil or charcoal stick. When you have exhausted your memory, open the book to examine the painting you love. Congratulations, you now know more about this painting than all of your classmates. Perform this little investigative procedure with other pictures, even if it takes copying a particular section of a picture. This does not mean you're a copycat. It means you want to learn how to compose your own art.

The library will have simplified books on drawing. Try to draw one small object. It may help to have a light on one side, so you can see the form better. If you still can't draw an object well enough, copy a drawing out of the art book and it may help you understand how to compose your drawing.

It is important to draw or paint one object on a paper rather than a whole scene that will screw you up and cause discouragement. One object well done can be more compelling than a contrived scene that may look amateurish. There is a tendency for many beginning artists to take on too much stuff in their pictures. The answer to producing great art is this: "Multiplicity in simplicity." If you don't know what this means, you're not alone so use the dictionary. If you do know what this means, employ this theory and it will put you ahead of the class. If I had learned how to use multiple effects within a monolithic work when I started out in art, I would have been ahead of the box.

Cowboy "Poker Players"
20 x 23 in. | Oil on canvas | By Hall Groat Sr. (age 15)
Painted over the top of a herd of sheep from circa 1880

HOW I COMPOSE A PAINTING

There are many ways to compose a painting and many artists develop personal approaches. I do not have a particular system. It depends on what I am trying to accomplish and the subject matter at hand.

In my early years, I would cover the entire surface with random tones of color and avoid establishing a definite theme. I would build my work from pure abstraction and just let it happen. If I discover a theme in my abstraction, I may try to enhance it and gradually bring it out. However, it may change several times before I establish subject matter with secondary shapes. This is an inventive way to paint if you're inclined to find order in disorder, although not recommended for an artist who finds comfort working academically.

Many years ago, I was doing a demonstration for The Thousand Islands Art Club. I used this highly inventive way to work, and I was on a roll when a gentleman blurted out in anger, "I disagree with the way you're doing this demonstration." I brushed off his comment to stay focused on my work. He also was quoted in the local newspaper with derogatory remarks regarding my aloofness to the art community. I was independently inclined so his remark was understandable.

Years later, Hans Junga, the gentleman critical of my demonstration, and I became friends—exchanged some prints, and went out to lunch together. He was a German and highly academic. In regard to our art, we were opposites. I am a Dutchman, and we were both stubborn in our approach to painting. The world of art is vast; there are a thousand ways to approach painting. Hans was very accomplished with his watercolor work taken from nature and had a definite look of his own.

Currently, I enjoy using an undertone that is allowed to show through and add brilliance to a painting. Sometimes bright yellow or red-rust tones permeate through my colors and help create a beautiful ambiance. I avoid developing a definite system and prefer to give each work a life of its own.

ORGANIZATION OF SUBJECT MATTER

When your painting is too busy you feel forced to eliminate important subject matter. By the same token, you hate to leave out the elements you want in your work. The problem may not be too much subject matter. There is no reason to assume you must eliminate one thing. Where is it written there is a limit to the amount of subject matter in a painting?

By organizing your composition, you can accommodate as much subject matter as you can imagine. This can be accomplished by using a tonal system of neutralizing parts of your composition, so subject matter can be suggested into quiet areas. Learning to push back subject matter and vary your size relationships will create room in your composition. You may need to decide which parts to pull to the foreground, because both size and tonal relationships are the key to a work of art with a large amount of objects.

Fifteen years ago I was commissioned to do a 30-by-40-inch acrylic painting for the Town of Geddes, near Syracuse. From this painting, a series of serigraph prints was produced and sold by the town. The original painting was framed and is permanently hung in the town office building. In my preliminary meetings with the town committee, the question arose about how many buildings I could put in the painting that would document the history of the town. My answer: "All of the buildings, including the New York State Fair." I had created a complex problem for myself, but I believed in my aforementioned statements. It turned out to be an incredible piece of art and was unveiled at a cocktail gala in the town office building.

LEARNING TO SEE TAKES PRACTICE

When you look at the great paintings of the world, it's a good idea to know how the artist leads your eye around his work. This is especially important for an artist who is studying how to make better art. One artist's work that comes to mind is Rembrandt's, especially his portraits. It's fun to watch people gazing upon the masters and to listen to their comments. A great portrait painter captures your eye through his ability to lead you through his composition. It's a good idea to know how an artist captures your attention with his work because it may heighten your appreciation and enable you to discriminate between greatness and mediocrity. There are many books that diagram composition and it may be a good idea to study them before you visit an art museum. This is especially important if you're a student in art school.

At the price of altering your notion of the grandeur found in the great portraits painted by Rembrandt, let me share some commonly heard comments of visitors at the National Gallery of Art in Washington, D.C., as they marveled at the portraits: "I love the way he paints the eyes of his subject. … I just can't stop staring at the expression on the old gentleman's face in the portrait. … He certainly captures the spirit of his subjects and my eyes are drawn to the face and the expression in his eyes. … She is such a beautiful woman in this Rembrandt portrait—I can see her spirit in her eyes."

How your eye is led to the center of interest in the painting is worth understanding and may take study. It is a good idea to look at other parts of a great painting and attempt to discover what brought your attention to this final crescendo—that tiny highlight in the eye that captures the viewer. And you better know why—especially if you're an art student.

Rembrandt van Rijn was born in 1606 in Leiden. He never traveled more than sixty miles from Amsterdam and, judging by his thousands of drawings, etchings, and countless paintings and self-portraits, he would not have had time. He was a dedicated artist and considered the greatest in history. Sorry Vermeer, but he produced much more art than you. They are two of my favorite painters in history. After visiting art museums all over Europe, I can think of no other artists greater than these two Dutchmen. I am proud to have at least one small Rembrandt etching in my collection. Vermeer was less prolific than Rembrandt, although arguably the best in the opinion of some art critics.

My wife, Rosemarie, and I traveled the world visiting major art museums. It was our hobby, and being an educator, she always read the titles and details on each piece of art. As aforementioned in my "early years," I am a lazy reader. I just studied the pictures and rarely took time to read the curatorial messages. She also read everything available about each country we visited. Later in life, we seemed to enjoy reading and discussing the same books. However, I seemed to look at the pictures first. I suppose that is my natural inclination. I do not read novels, but love history and anthropology. I consider myself a victim of the age of specialization, although the late Anna Olmsted, who wrote art reviews for *The Post-Standard* for many years, characterized me as "a peripatetic painter." She had me dead to rights in that review. I believe artist Jan De Ruth was aware of my jumping from one subject to another in my art. Historians dislike artists who do not work in series, as they are harder to write about.

In studying art in museums, my son, Hall II, and I took the Amtrak to Chicago one year to review the work at the Chicago Institute of Art and other galleries. We enjoyed the Peter Paul Ruben works and discussed his use of color to great extent. How to make Ruben's red is a mystery and perhaps a lost art. I was surprised to see portraits by Ivan Albright, whose creations were used for the first movie I saw as a kid—*The Picture of Dorian Gray*. He was one wacky artist I will never forget, with his ghoulish portraits. This was the first movie performance for actress Angela Lansbury, an Academy Award winner.

We did Chicago on foot and took in the highlights, but returned to the institute and went through the collection a second time. The guard said, "You guys do not need another ticket— glad to see you back." On this viewing, we met David Hockney, who was preparing for his one-man show. On our return trip to Syracuse my son ran into an old classmate and we had a great beer party on Amtrak. Learning to see is an ongoing dedication for an artist, and being on a train, studying industrial complexes along the way, provides ideas for one of my favorite subjects to paint—railroad yards.

On one of our three trips to the UK, my wife and I went through the National Portrait Museum, British Museum, The Tate and several others. However, it was the work of contemporary German painter Lucian Freud that has stayed with me the longest. He was the grandson of Sigmund Freud, and perhaps that explains his sex-crazed subject matter. In my humble opinion, Lucian Freud was one of the world's best figure painters. The visceral quality in his brushwork is loaded with emotion and the stark nakedness of his subjects can only be excused by his tremendous power as a painter. I'm still learning to see, and studying art is an ongoing passion for a working artist.

Village in Antwerp
21 x 14 in. | Watercolor | By Hall Groat Sr. (age 16)

FINDING THE QUALITIES THAT DEFINE YOUR ART

Nothing is more elusive than your own art. After years of painting and experimenting with different approaches in painting, you may overlook the handwriting that defines your art. Let's consider the notion that your life as an artist is one big painting. Obviously if you don't experiment, you will never grow as a painter. But somehow, a painter can lose sight of the most defining characteristics that make his art unique. Artists can be identified by their brush marks, colors, or special way of composing a picture, which becomes their signature style. Perhaps the way you approach your new work doesn't materialize into a successful effort after several years. Your attempt to re-establish your identity in search of improvement is disappointing. This is a normal process to go through in painting, but you may decide to return to your original style. All the experimenting has not been in vain as you revert back to your earlier way of working. You will bring all the insight gained and you may become a better painter. Those qualities that define your art will be better realized. What seemed elusive to you may now become crystal clear and you will be empowered by your experience.

THE EVOLUTION OF MY PAINTING PROCESS

Watercolor painting comes very easy to me. For some reason, I prefer to work in a heavy impasto where the surface of the painting is built up with various materials to create an interesting texture to work on. After a gesso priming, I sometimes used modeling paste or even fabrics sealed in an acrylic gel with a sand-like material embedded into the surface. For many years, I worked on Masonite and later luan board or illustration board for smaller works. On many of my early works I would paint non-objectively for an hour or so, before I even considered subject matter. I would wait until my surface provided inspiration to create an impression of some nebulous subject. But if it didn't, I would be content if I ended up with a non-objective work. Surface is everything in painting and if I'm not happy with the surface and the way the paint feels, it's time to leave the studio and hit some balls at Green Lakes golf course.

It was a gradual process in developing the kind of art I enjoy doing. I tried many different looks before evolving into what became my signature style. By using unconventional painting tools, I was able the employ the painting style that related to the drawing style I developed at sixteen. A few painters of the late 1950s experimented with spatulas and razor blades as alternative painting tools, including William Palmer, director of the Munson-Williams-Proctor

Arts Institute in Utica, Gordon Steele, Homer Roy Martin (later Holm Martin) and John Boison. We all had success in our work.

Many of my works during this period suggested industrial subjects and railroads with boxcars. There was no overt attempt to illustrate or paint these boxcars in a literal way. Through suggestion, I could seduce viewers into believing they were seeing the railroad yards. I may have alluded to a particular subject, but viewers had to interpret my work in their own way. I discovered the suggestion was more powerful than the reality. For years people would write to me about finding things in my paintings they had never seen before, even several years after the purchase.

The time was ripe to market art and my career was on a roll. My painting is never exactly the same from day to day, as I try to give each work its individual life. By doing this, my mind stays fresh and avoids becoming arid. I don't believe that getting into a formula in painting leads to anything other than imitating yesterday's success. Each day offers a chance for self-discovery and you grow every day, although it may not be detectable. I believe it takes courage to lay it on the line and work out of a preconceived notion of what your art is about. Nothing you learn gets wasted. The more ways you paint, the more you increase your ability to rescue that ho-hum painting. An example: I mentioned my watercolor work in my teens and early twenties. Even today, at any given time, I may pick up a flat sable brush and use it to glaze in areas of a painting with the freedom and confidence of an experienced watercolorist. It's important to try something you can't do, because if you don't try, you will never know for sure. The fear of failure will hold you back from reaching your optimum skill level. Your art can be studied just as a graphologist deciphers personality traits in your handwriting. If you're a tight and inhibited artist, your work will reveal those hang-ups, and you will be condemned to third-rate status until you get a shot of courage. No artist ever got to the top playing it safe. Lately I have been working in oil on canvas and prefer to stand at either a French drawing table or an easel, depending on the size of my painting.

After painting for sixty-five years, I am on cruise control and can now talk on the phone, watch television, or listen to the Syracuse Symphony Orchestra, and still have success while painting. In fact, if I really want to get inspired for another great work, I just listen to the SSO directed by Maestro Daniel Hege while I paint. That works for me.

CHANGING YOUR THEME IN MIDSTREAM

Sometimes a painting gets away from you and you no longer have any feeling for the theme. It happens to me often and I just transform it into something else. This is done easily when your oil paint is still tacky. However, when the paint sets up, you must sand the surface and remove any unwanted ridges of paint. Many great works throughout history are over older paintings and, with modern technology, the original work can be revealed. There is no need to throw away unwanted art that isn't up to your level of expectation. With a little sandpaper you can make changes to an unfinished work midstream, or long after finishing. Quite often the under painting provides an interesting surface to work on, providing you're not a photo realist painter. Impressionist painters often enjoy working on irregular surfaces where there is a little paint build-up. Your work may end up having more character.

THE SELECTION OF SUBJECT MATTER

When breaking into the art world it is important to paint subject matter that removes you from common ideas that exploit a young artist. *American Artist* could be considered ordinary as an art magazine. Your taste is molded by what you see, read, hear about and assume is a direction to fulfillment in life. Certainly this is true in music as well. Our ears are bombarded daily by commercially produced music that sells. Every second sound-mixers and composers are taking what they know to be marketable and turning those ideas into music. Society's desire to conform ensures mediocrity will prevail. Early exposure to the classics is a way to avoid this and can broaden your perception in all art forms. Changing the station on your radio can liberate you from the ordinary to the extraordinary. For example, news stations like NPR offer you a less politically motivated slant on world affairs. Our lives are being molded like a piece of clay. Each day we allow input from lower forms of art, music, and information about our world, we lessen the opportunity for fulfillment.

My painting professor at Syracuse University once stated that easel painting is dead. Fortunately he was wrong. That was in the mid-fifties and I'm still "slinging the brush." Technology does offer infinite ways to be creative. There are a zillion painters still working, but only 2 percent have any fresh ideas. The great painter Cézanne escaped the contemporary traps of his time by hiking up to the mountains to paint his own legacy. The artist who realizes great art comes from original ideas is part of that 2 percent who are the leaders in the field.

I have often been asked, "How does your subject matter reveal itself to you?" Decisions about what I paint are offered in my environment by aesthetic enticement. A fleeting sun ray that touches the edge of a given object may inspire by capturing the eye for a millisecond. The study of aesthetics broadens your ability to feel your subject, as well as perceive it. Feeling and emotion are the best way to interpret the aesthetics of art. Through letting yourself become one with nature, instead of making a critical selection, you can discover the beauty of the universe. This allows your creative mind to reach beyond a preconceived notion of what you want to paint or what you believe is important to record in art.

An artist who has the most sensitivity to his environment is the truly gifted one. The human mind is like a songbird—when inside a cage it becomes repetitive and ceases to discover new music in life. My selections in art subject matter arrive as a belated form of illumination on the pathway to self-actualization.

UNDERSTANDING YOUR OWN ART

The most elusive and difficult art to understand is an artist's own work. We know so little about ourselves, and in time become only a caricature of the person we claim to be. A mirror introduces us to a reverse image that may or may not flatter our egos. We go through life with only an impression of what we look like. Some people fall in love with their image, while others may choose cosmetic surgery. Perhaps this may be why an artist decides to hide away in a world of fantasy and create art that puts him in touch with his inner feelings. It is not unusual for an artist to escape from society and seek comfort in being reclusive.

There are many artists who will not show their work. Some may have low self-esteem, while others choose not to share their artwork with a world they find no comfort in. We often characterize them as shy or super-sensitive. However, mental illness is not uncommon in artists, and the great Vincent van Gogh was driven to suicide by his demons.

It is extremely complex to understand why an artist's work takes on a particular look of its own. Just what makes your handwriting different than that of others is also a mystery. Perhaps it is impossible to understand your own art any more than you understand your genetic make-up. How my own paintings have transformed over sixty years is a question I will attempt to deal with. I can remember the first painting I saw upon entering the Metropolitan Museum in New York. It was a very small oil of a boat by Albert Pinkham Ryder. I was about fifteen. I saw it as too simplistic to be in the museum, but now realize the significance of this monolithic composition. Why this work stays in my memory is hard to explain. Perhaps it's like a bad song lodged in my brain to irritate through repetitiveness.

American art has always held my interest. The artists known as "The Eight" who were active from 1908-1918 and became part of "The Ash Can School" are more in keeping with my personality. Railroad trains, the Bowery, and the dark side of life inspired my early paintings. This is suggested in much of my art of the '60s and '70s. As a kid, I bummed around in the same environment that appeared in my early work. At sixteen I hitchhiked to Manhattan and ended up in the Garment District—took a nickel subway ride to Coney Island and later hung out on the docks in lower Manhattan. It was as if I were walking in the footsteps of George Bellows.

While lecturing at the Savannah School of Art and Design twenty years ago, I took time to visit the Telfair Museum and requested a viewing of one of Bellows' best Hudson River paintings. It was removed from the storage racks, and I was allowed to examine it from front to back, in detail. When a piece of art means this much to me, I like to handle it. The director realized its significance to me, and was receptive to my requests. Early exposure in those impressionable years had much to do with my development as an artist. Being inspired by particular paintings has helped motivate my career. I suppose it's only natural to move in the direction you identify with. Although my work is diverse in subject matter, I find industrial subjects to be the most compelling.

WAR CAN INSPIRE AN ARTIST

We all know that Francis Scott Key penned the lyrics to *The Star-Spangled Banner* during the War of 1812. But the fact remains that even in the horrors of war when soldiers are blown to bits, there is still beauty in the night skies. If this was not the case, we wouldn't be watching the fireworks on the Fourth of July and many other celebrations.

From our trench line at Outpost Easy during the Korean War, the night skies were incredibly beautiful as streams of tracer bullets and machine-gun fire raked the enemy. Our aircraft pilots would fly over the North Koreans and napalm bombs would leave the mountainside an inferno. Enemy soldiers were incinerated by the thousands as the red glow from the tremendous heat became indelible in your memory. Perhaps the famous painting *Dante's Inferno* illustrates this vision of horror as well.

GRAPHOLOGY AND ART

Handwriting analysis can be fun and it has been a hobby of mine for many years. It's a great way of getting to know people at parties and can break the ice with introverted people. When I meet an artist, however, his artwork is more revealing than the handwriting. Some personality types are often predictable. Engineers or mathematicians tend to be pragmatic and write in a clear unpretentious way. People with strong personalities tend to write bold and direct. My wife, Rosemarie, wrote in a large and bold way; that didn't surprise me as she had an out-front personality with strong character. Doctors tend to write in disguise, judging by the prescriptions they write. It may be more of an affectation or code between them and pharmacists. I believe doctors write as well as anyone else, but prefer not to reveal their true identities—at least not to this graphologist. People in the arts are more sensitive about their writing and some develop great signatures that are collectibles. Karen Gaul Mills, former executive director of the Syracuse Symphony Orchestra, has a signature that could be used by a jewelry designer for a pendant. It's gorgeous.

There are tendencies for certain psychotic people to express hostility in their signatures. Adolf Hitler had strong handwriting and his signature ended in a sharp down stroke. My father had the same heavy down stroke and a very strong signature. My own signature varies from day to day. I have one style that I use to sign my artwork and another with documents. Sometimes I switch my "G" from lower case to upper case. Banks have called me in on this in their vigilance to catch forgers. I also switch from script to printing quite often. Penmanship took a dive with the advent of the ballpoint. Good handwriting is becoming a lost art. When I see the way students these days hold a pen or pencil, it's amazing they can write at all.

DRAWING WITHOUT SIGHT IS POSSIBLE

Many years ago my wife and I were attending a modern dance program at Jacob's Pillow in the Berkshires. I had a drawing pad and pencil sitting on my lap and was eager to do some action sketches of the dancers. When the program started and the house lights were off, I realized it was a foolish idea—or was it? The choreography and music were inspirational and I started sketching with emphasis on the leaping motion of the performers. My eyes were glued to the performance, as my sketches were done in complete darkness. At intermission I looked at my sketches while enjoying a glass of wine with Rosemarie. It turned out to be a good idea, as the sketches captured the spirit of the dancers and I had interpreted the first act accurately. Returning from the event, I was puzzled how I could have done these drawings without seeing the drawing paper, and soon it came together for me. As an undergraduate fine art major at Syracuse University, I took a lecture course given by Professor Bill Hart in aesthetics. He had done some drawings on the board illustrating to the class how simple suggestive lines, although incomplete, would make sense in conjunction with other lines that complete the picture. Now that the reader is thoroughly confused, let me present another experiment that will be your key to understanding. Bill would print a word on the board, but by eliminating portions of each letter left the class in the dark about what the word was. Someone would eventually call out the word, or if not, one tiny additional line told the story. This illustrates how minimal lines or suggestions can communicate an idea, an emotion, or a whole picture. The kinesthetic reaction you get at that millisecond of comprehension is that magical power of suggestion.

The Greenhouse
30 x 40 in. | Oil on canvas | By Hall Groat Sr.

PAINTING IN THE RAIN

When you look back on your career and try to recall a special time of pleasure, it seems strange to remember a rainy day as one of your fondest experiences. Few artists would consider standing out in the rain entertaining, and many would forgo our experience twenty years ago at North Truro, Cape Cod. My son, Hall II, and I decided to take a painting trip during his college break. Rosemarie also went along and we all enjoyed being together for a short vacation. We set up our easels on the bluffs overlooking the bay at North Truro. The sky was overcast and the forecast was rain. Rosemarie elected to sit in the car with a book, as she felt there were enough painters in the family. As the sky darkened, our brushes moved quickly. Fortunately, my son and I were working on small boards in oil. We knew we were in for a drenching, but I knew he would brave any weather for the sake of art. I was the only one with a rain jacket. I offered it to him, although I knew he would be too macho to accept it. We worked intensely and painted similar subjects. We both were rain soaked, but too riveted in our painting to be concerned. I enjoyed painting old cottages that appeared abandoned by their owners. Looking down from my easel into a hedgerow of wild roses, I spotted additional subject matter that appeared as an interesting composition—Wallace Bassford's Art School. By coincidence, I had met Wally a few years earlier at his Palm Beach Art School, right off Worth Avenue. He had invited me in to watch him do a demonstration for his society ladies. All these memories went through my head as I attempted to keep the rain drops off my eyeglasses. Having some connection with your subject matter also helps in finding success in your art. My son and I each did a bunch of paintings and the oil paint repelled the rain. We lined them in the back of our vehicle, headed back to the Mainstay Motor Inn and got into some dry clothes. The early lobster dinner at the Whitman House followed a dry martini that capped off a perfect day of painting in the rain.

DRAWING CAN BE A GOOD DISTRACTION FOR AN ARTIST

As far back as I can remember I have used drawing as a distraction from uncomfortable situations. I like drawing, but my joy as an artist is centered on painting. One brush stroke can take the place of hundreds of lines in sketching. As a painter, I like to create art built up from simplified brush strokes. As Josef Albers said, "Do less and get more," and this works for me. However, there remain certain situations where drawing is my only recourse. When I was as young as three years old, my mother would put paper and pencil before me to keep me occupied in waiting rooms or while visiting her friends.

On Sundays my mother would take me to church. I always reached for a pencil and did drawings on the church programs. My subject was usually the backs of people's heads in the sanctuary. In those days women wore hats and I could catch a likeness with ease. I became very proficient in sketching people from the back. My mother was proud of my drawings of people she knew and would often hand them a sketch. There were a few great ministers who eventually commanded my attention and their sermons were inspirational. However, if

I was seen sketching, it usually revealed my boredom. Every Sunday morning I would ask my mother who the church soloist was. If it was Alan Sanderson, I was sure to go. He was a baritone who I enjoyed hearing. Alan became a casual friend and we worked out with barbells together. He went on to be in Broadway musical productions, and our careers took different directions.

However, sketching while attending a symphony is not a distraction; it's my deliberate reaction to inspirational music, and I feel driven to record the orchestra in performance. I never took my sketching seriously until former Syracuse Symphony Orchestra executive director Karen Gaul Mills spotted some sketches on the symphony program that I carried into the intermission party. She asked if I would donate them to the symphony for publication and I was delighted to do so. In retrospect, sketching in church as a kid with a captive congregation used for models was beneficial in my becoming an artist. I was careful to sit where I would not disturb anyone and always used discretion.

Waiting to be served in restaurants also presents a great opportunity to sketch. Many folks have asked for sketches that include them and I usually oblige. One day my brother Rod and I went for a beer on Westcott Street and I started sketching people at the bar on napkins. Rod wanted the people to have a sketch by me. They, in turn, had the bartender set up beers for us. It was great fun to witness their expressions and hear comments from their friends.

Recently, I had to wait at the motor vehicle bureau to renew my driver's license. It was sad to see people sitting idle with sour expressions, waiting for their number to be posted. I put those dead moments to good use with my sketching, and avoided wasting time in idleness.

MY SIGNATURE PLACEMENT

When I started painting in the late forties I signed my work by my last name only, in the lower left- or right-hand corner. After a few years, I signed only my first name. I soon decided to sign vertically in the lower left-hand corner, but made a sudden bold decision to sign my name where I had never seen any other artist sign his work: in the upper left-hand corner. For the past forty-eight years I have used mainly a brush script "Hall Groat" and the date, and with rare exceptions have kept it there. On some of my large murals I have signed down at the bottom so it could be read with more ease.

In 1970 the Wellfleet Gallery called and asked me to sign my works in a conventional place. But the director, Thomas Gaglione, changed his mind at the urging of Xavier Gonzalez, who also exhibited at the gallery. Another gallery complained about the fact that I dated my work.

They felt that if a work didn't sell after a few years, potential customers would feel that perhaps it wasn't good enough. I went along with this for a few years, until Haden Patten, a personal friend and collector of my art, complained to me that he wanted to see those dates so he could track my progress in art. Haden was astute to pick up on this and it now annoys me to see some of my older works undated.

SELF-EMPLOYMENT AS AN ARTIST

Many people have asked me how I knew when to become self-employed. A sudden change would have been disastrous, as you need cash flow to exist. Being employed in the art field by a company rarely offers much opportunity for advancement. I have always had to work on art sales on the side to exist.

When my art sales became equal to what I earned as a salaried employee, I knew I could make the break. However, first you must be debt free and have enough cash to exist for a year. I also had to be prepared to work twelve-hour days, or all night if necessary. Once that point was reached, I knew I could devote myself full time to my art career and increase my income way beyond what I could have made working for a company in my field. But I also realized I would have to be responsible for every phase of my business. I loved it all. I knew if I had to pay for custom framing and a sales representative, my profit would dwindle, if there was any profit at all. Most artists I have talked to claim they dislike the idea of doing their own sales. Those people would have a difficult time as self-employed artists.

I don't believe I could duplicate my career that started in the 1960s. I had a professor at Syracuse University who told the class that if you can paint beautiful women, you could make money. These days it doesn't matter if you can paint beautiful women, babies, children, family groupings or animal portraits. Someone has to market the work and if you lack that ability, you need to find another job.

PRICING ARTWORK

There are many ways to set the price of your artwork. Some artists use trial and error, but this is often a deceiving method because if you don't sell, you assume your work is overpriced. The opposite may be true, because if your work is under priced, potential buyers may think it isn't good enough to buy. If an artist is uncomfortable selling his own work, this may send a signal to a potential buyer that he lacks self-worth or doesn't believe in his own product. The most common way a new artist prices his or her work is to see how others price their work. That may be a mistake because you're sending a signal that you're incapable of making an intelligent evaluation of your own work. Many artists feel the price should reflect the hours put into their work. Unfortunately, the amateur artist is generally slower than the professional, so the hourly method becomes moot. If you were selecting a surgeon for a life-threatening procedure, you would not pick a slow one. You could die on the operating table. A painting can die at the hands of an incompetent artist as well, by being overworked. The paint can be rubbed and muddled to a point that the painting loses its life and the colors turn to mud. An artist breaking into the art world years ago told me his method of pricing his acrylic paintings. He said he merely copied his prices off my work of a comparable size. When I asked why, he said his work was as good as mine. I would have had more respect for him had he said his work was better than mine and made his prices higher. He had a limited career that was cut short by an untimely death. Pricing by ego has its drawbacks, too. If you feel you're the best in your field, you may be in for a rude awakening, because an inflated ego can give you a false sense of superiority. You may set your prices too high and experience a lack of sales. The more exposure you have in the art world, the more you will find your personal price line. It's an ongoing process that every artist must deal with.

PAINTING BY NUMBERS

Many wannabe painters needed some way to produce art, so a clever system was produced, packaged and promoted fifty years ago—"Paint by Numbers." It allowed people to have instant success and sets were sold in every art store and hobby shop in America. This idea caught the imagination of thousands of people who felt empowered to paint pictures.

During the 1960s, I was a frequent guest on TV shows. Phil Markert was the host at Channel 9 in Shoppingtown Mall in DeWitt. He fielded questions by phone for me to comment on. One call was from a WWII veteran who wanted my opinion on the "painting-by-numbers" craze. My answer was simple and geared to improve the process of "painting-by-numbers" enthusiasts.

"After you have completed your numbers or finished your painting, blend each number together with its neighbor number—this should result in a more natural looking work."

Many paint-by-numbers hobbyists were outraged and called the TV show with their complaints. One advocated I was promoting "cheating by the numbers." It all seems very bizarre as I look back on this naïve time in history.

PEOPLE IN THE RELATED ARTS HAVE THE SAME DILEMMA

The most common complaint I hear from people in the world of art and music is their lives are a financial struggle. There are many artists and musicians who have extraordinary skill; however, only a miniscule are able to make a living. Painters rarely have peace of mind. The bills roll in much quicker than the art goes out. It is irresponsible to enter into fine arts if you want a family and enjoy what life has to offer. In today's economy there is hardly time left to pursue your creative pleasures. Every minute of each day seems to be dominated by a need to produce more funds to survive.

One of the problems is the stereotypical image that society seems to hold over people in the arts. If you want to lift yourself out of the role that society expects of you, your peers may reference you as too commercial and not a true artist. A sociological trap keeps an artist from finding the good life for his family. The desire to have friends and colleagues in your field seems natural. But "misery loves company" and ultimately you must find your own way out of the dilemma. There is a way out of the "starving artist image." If I didn't believe that, I would not be in this field. I hope my manuscript may shed some light on the subject. The greatest accomplishment you will ever achieve is the financial freedom to pursue life in the arts. If it's truly your life's passion—go for it and remember it's very crowded at the bottom. At the top, the competition thins out enough for you to see your pathway to freedom of expression.

TIME IS THE ONLY TEST FOR SUCCESS IN ART

When a new painting is finished and you're convinced it's good, you have to put it aside before passing final judgment. Far too many times I have been fooled by my own art. Sometimes I have been too quick to pass judgment and considered it a loser, only to find I had ruined a good painting by trying to rescue it. It's sad to lose a new painting because you failed to recognize its qualities. It's much easier to judge art created by someone else because you can be objective and are not involved in another artist's mental process. How you feel about your own painting may be based on your experience with the subject at hand. Very often a painter may have a preconceived notion about the subject at hand and paint from memory rather than letting the creative process take place. When the subject matter you're working on becomes more important than the painting process, you can become robotic and cease to be creative. A case in point is my large oil of sea grass that I have been studying for three months. Yesterday, I decided it was a "big bore," and I would not honor it on my wall for another day. I transformed it into a lily pond. Wow—it looks great! But now I must set it aside for a few weeks to see whether it survives the test of time.

EARLY EXPOSURE TO ART MUSEUMS

Sometimes when a youth walks through a museum and glances at the artwork on exhibit he may appear bored. After all, most kids want to be outside playing with friends. Many kids may be obsessed with sports and if parents drag them to a museum, they may appear disinterested. Don't assume the kids are bored, as something you're unaware of may catch their interest. Invariably, they may retain information in a subliminal way and at some point a curious remark about the museum will surface. Kids often assimilate more than we realize.

Going through the Louvre in Paris, I overheard a young boy remark about the large figurative works to his parents. When the youngster was asked his opinion about the paintings, he said, "All the feet on these soldiers are too big." It was an interesting observation because these paintings of warriors were all at least ten feet high. The young boy was not over three-and- a-half feet tall. Therefore, from his eye level, the feet appeared too large in perspective. It was a valid point.

Developing discriminating tastes in art-related topics is important, and early exposure through visits to museums provides the enrichment required in becoming a sophisticated adult. Throughout your lifetime you may carry information assimilated through exposure to the related arts. Every day, we take for granted decisions about color selections. For example, a shopper in a clothing store may make decisions based on early exposure. Deciding which color fits into her wardrobe or complements her looks is learned. Infinite experiences in life are enriched by the development of discriminating taste in the arts. This starts in childhood and is enhanced by early exposure.

LEARNING TO FINISH

If your painting becomes laborious, you're undoubtedly doing something wrong. Making artwork is supposed to be fun; however, if you're struggling to no avail, join the club— every artist wrestles with this issue. You may be trying too hard, which may be counterproductive; instead, be the boss and don't let your painting control you. Back off a little and loosen up until you can work your way back into your painting. Sometimes it's a good idea to bounce off of a second piece and switch back and forth until something clicks in your head and you see the light. Putting your art away and just giving up may be a cowardly way to deal with it. I used to give up in the middle, too. But when I had a rack filled with too many unfinished works it became depressing. I spent a whole year without starting a new work of art, and dedicated my entire effort to rescuing unfinished paintings. I became so astute in this process I learned to enjoy what was agonizing before. Learning to finish well is a better test of your ability than merely starting a painting. Now, when I find a painting in my studio that needs finishing, I accept the challenge of forcing myself to resolve the painting, which is empowering.

MULTIPLICITY WITHIN SIMPLICITY

In observing many amateur painters work, it becomes apparent they often take on too much subject matter. Too much going on in your painting can prevent you from reaching your optimum level of success. One object can be enough to start with in a still life, or a single tree and not the whole forest. The more subject matter you tackle, the more amateurish your work may look. Believe me, I know. I was studying with Josef Albers, who was a world-famous artist from the Bauhaus School. He stood behind me as I painted and said, "You have a tendency to be too busy—do less and get more—Americans don't understand how to simplify." He referenced the American Cadillac, when it had the big tail fins in the early fifties. He asked, "What does all that extra stuff have to do with good design? Tail fins or fin tails are non-functional and ugly." That being said, it's not easy to be simple—but bear in mind that "multiplicity within simplicity" is your key to creating great art.

NATURE TEACHES COMPOSITION BEST

World travel offers a unique opportunity to witness breathtaking sights. Understanding what you see and why this vision may stay with you for a lifetime is important to an artist. In reviewing my travels alone and later with my wife, many incredible scenes were witnessed. Everyone is exposed to the beauty around them and many take it for granted. However, artists may train their eye to interpret the grandeur of nature, as well as its aesthetic composition. Many artists develop a heightened sense of reality, with the ability to analyze subject matter for use in their painting. Certainly, this is true with a painter or a professional photographer. Answering questions about the basic design elements becomes second nature to an artist. What is found in the foreground, middle ground or background in a scene is organized with ease. They may look for lines of opposition to create power in their composition. The negative and positive shapes and the juxtaposition of one form to another are mandatory considerations. The temperature of a painting is also important in selecting your color pallet. The list could go on eternally, as nature is in constant transition. Painters who work from nature develop the skill to adapt to changes in lighting. Those who use photos for reference have an easier time, although they may miss out on the spiritual connection to the environment and subject. Serious painters experience many ways of interpreting their subject matter, even if it entails painting out in inclement weather.

Alaska, from the deck of my troop ship in the army, was a view to long remember. As the ship entered the inland sound, the waters were calm, offering relief from a previous storm at sea. Northwest of Vancouver was the worst weather of the trip and being on deck was the best place to hang out, as most seasick soldiers stayed below in their bunks. The midnight sun and the northern lights created an unusual aura. It was spring and melting shards of ice were sliding into the sea. The air was clear and you could see a hundred miles, as if it were a short distance away. The violet and turquoise colors of icebergs reflected in the deep blue waters were enhanced by the salt air. As a painter, I found inspiration and a desire to capture these subjects on canvas. Although the *Marine Phoenix* was hardly a recreational ship, seeing Alaska from its deck offered a look into the wonders of nature.

Sailing through inland waters near Sasebo, Japan, revealed a dazzling display of lights reflecting everywhere. Hospital ships with giant red crosses were a reminder that in a few days Korea was my next trip and possibly a one-way journey. Cargo ships, naval ships, Japanese fishing boats, and lights from distant hillside homes and gardens covered every inch of land. I was mesmerized by the beauty of this harbor at night. Years later, I was able to recall this scene in my watercolor paintings. Beauty of this magnitude, you never forget, and many of my watercolor works are built around the suggestion of the port of Sasebo.

Switzerland offered another type of visual excitement. The most beautiful city on a lake I have ever seen is Lucerne. Unfortunately my wife, Rosemarie, and I were only there for two days. The city is like a jewel and the Swiss keep it pristine with immaculate homes. I later did some acrylic paintings of beautiful homes by the water. Winding through the Alps is an unnerving experience in a tour bus. The drop-offs were literally thousands of feet down. Hundreds of mountain waterfalls were very inviting as subject matter for my painting. Working in a vertical format can be challenging to a painter. I have been conditioned to a conventional type of countryside at home in Manlius. It takes a while to orient yourself to extreme vertical compositions as seen in the Alps.

The Matterhorn can be a challenge to see. When we checked into our lodge, a few tourists said they were unable to see the mountain and left disappointed. On our second morning in the

Alps, I looked out the window and only saw billowing clouds. I stood staring for a long while, but realized I was not looking up high enough. Straight up overhead, the clouds finally parted for about ten seconds. That famous scene of the peak of the Matterhorn appeared, and soon disappeared. Later in the day it returned to stay for the rest of our trip. I did some small color studies of this majestic mountain. When you paint a picture of something, you also record it in your memory. Years later I painted it in different views with cloud formations in my Manlius studio. This mountain has a distinctive shape unlike any other I have seen. Some of these works were sold a few years ago to a Chicago collector.

The Hale-Bopp Comet offered the most unusual sighting, witnessed by Rosemarie from her window seat on our flight to Europe. It was 1997 and sixty-five-year-old Marshall Applewhite, head of Heaven's Gate, a religious cult, had just finished leading his thirty-nine members into a suicide pact and exodus from earth by following the comet. By coincidence, my nephew Stuart Grauer, owner of The Grauer School in San Diego, along with wife Sally, had been dining at a San Diego sports bar, just prior to this horrific tragedy. Stuart told me, " Sally and I didn't realize who these people were at the time, but observed the strange group at a long table, looking somber, and dressed in new matching black Nike sportswear. All these men and women also wore matching white sneakers. There were at least twelve at their seating." After dinner they left, and Marshall Applewhite escorted the first of three groups to Rancho Santa Fe where Heaven's Gate had leased a room. As a cult leader skilled in the art of persuasion, Applewhite knew the group had complete faith in him and indoctrinated them into believing the world would end soon. Their only salvation was to exit earth in their vessel—meaning their spirit after death—which was required to transport them to a new world. He explained that after death they would trail behind the Hale-Bopp Comet and orbit to a new world. Each person packed one matching black piece of luggage to accompany the vessel away from the doomed earth, and to a better life. Each member took phenobarbital as a poison, followed by a chaser of vodka. A back-up person was on hand to place a plastic bag over their heads, ensuring death by suffocation. A matching purple shroud was placed upon each member's chest, as proper attire for their earthly exodus. This process was repeated for three evenings, until all members, including Applewhite, were dead. It was many days later before the thirty-nine corpses were discovered in their Rancho Santa Fe room. Investigators were awestruck on how neat the bodies were laid out. Applewhite had orchestrated a mass suicide while still able to leave the room immaculate. After Rosemarie spotted the comet, she called me to the airplane window, but I was too late to catch a glimpse of Hale-Bopp in orbit over our aircraft. I missed the opportunity to wave farewell to the Heaven's Gate vessels trailing the comet.

TWO JUDGES FOR ART SHOW? BAD IDEA

The Sarasota Art Association on Tamiami Trail, Florida, decided on two judges for its annual art competition—and I was one of them. The three categories were watercolor, oil and sculpture. My co-judge, Valfred Thelin, and I went through the entries and took notes. Several of the watercolor entries were by his workshop students. We agreed on many of the selections, with one exception. We had made our picks independently for the awards; however, in the category of sculpture, we had opposite reactions to the work. Valfred took a strong stand on his selection and I disagreed. I had selected a piece of sculpture he did not care for. After discussing these two works for a considerable length of time, it became apparent we were hopelessly deadlocked. Valfred suggested we eliminate the award for sculpture. I agreed and when we informed Virginia, the president of the association, she expressed displeasure. The art association members who were entered in the sculpture category were understandably angered. Two judges for an art show is a bad idea as it takes three to break a deadlock.

NOT IN THE MOOD AND UNINSPIRED?

Many wannabe painters have a list of excuses why they don't get started in their art. Who can afford the luxury of inspiration in any career? Can you imagine what would happen if everyone in the workforce had to be in the mood or must wait for inspiration? No matter what you feel like before starting is meaningless; a painter must start working to get in the mood. Inspiration comes from involvement in the painting process. I have done my best work with back pain and no apparent desire to paint. There is something magical about creativity. It puts you in the mood and inspires you to tap into your inner strength.

THE AGONY AND THE ECSTASY OF COMMISSIONED WORK

It's wonderful when a patron or a corporation commissions a painting. It can be the highlight of your whole year and may bring in some needed funds. But sometimes it can be agonizing, depending on with whom you're dealing. My latest commission was a very rewarding experience. It came from a person who respected my ability as an artist and had the wisdom to know my complete freedom would produce the best results. The subject commissioned depicted a historic hotel and my customer knew I was inspired by the subject. It was a large vertical oil on canvas and there was never a question about my success with it. Working on this painting was pure ecstasy and even the difficult passages were fun to tackle. Completing this painting was the highlight of 2009.

However, when a customer dictates every detail wanted in a painting, including every color, and then requires changes to fit into a particular setting at the advice of an interior designer, it can inhibit you to a point of agony. It's best to not accept a commission that causes you to become depressed—life is too short.

EXAMINING SUITABILITY FOR SELF-EMPLOYMENT

Perhaps you should flip the page to the next story, but curiosity will undoubtedly prevail and keep you here. Let us first examine the type of person you are. You may not be suitable for a life of self-employment in anything. And if that's the case, art is probably the worst choice. However, if you don't mind catching meals in the soup kitchen and hoofing it, rather than trying to own a car with no gas money, art may be a good choice after all. In all probability, you will soon be searching for steady work, and be much happier in a field that pays a decent salary.

Being with other people in an office is important for most people. You may enjoy those company parties where you can swoon over the boss's secretary, while waiting for your raise that never seems to get approved—hmm? Seriously, self-employment can be a very lonely life—especially in art. The nature of creative art is one of introspection, and people around you may be a distraction. However, you will be able to accomplish more than someone pushing papers in an office. Your hours are your own and you call all the shots. When I look out my front window, holding a hot cup of coffee on those below-zero mornings, I'm thankful I'm no longer in that rush-hour traffic. I'm already at work and my boss is that great guy I see in the mirror every morning. The opportunity for you to make a decent living is your choice. No one will hold your hand. If you lack self-discipline, discontinue any plans of self-employment in art. However, if you're highly motivated, independently inclined, with a good track record in sales… whoops! Did I say sales? Most people are turned off with the idea of doing their own sales. It would be too demeaning to sell your own artwork. How could you ask someone to buy your paintings? You could show your work to a gallery, which could sell it for you. Galleries would only take 50 percent—that's if anyone wants to buy your stuff. Of course, there are many artists much better than you, so you will need to be patient to make a sale. Who is going to frame your art if you're a painter? A custom framer will cost you a bundle so there goes your profit. If the gallery gives that special customer a discount, you may be working at a loss. Better learn every phase of your profession and also know how to do your own framing. If you're squeamish about plugging your own work or making cold calls when you start out, you're not a candidate for self-employment. In fact, most companies would not want a wimp as an employee either. If you're a terrific artist and incredible at sales, and find that what you do is marketable, by all means go for it. You can put away your alarm clock, because being late for work should no longer be a concern. However, you may be driven to work longer hours than people employed by companies. That may be because you're finally happy being self-employed as an artist, and for the first time in your adult life—you are free.

CHAPTER 8

TIDBITS

AVENUE ART GALLERY IN ENDICOTT

A wonderful addition to Endicott, New York, was the transformation of a historic building into an art gallery that fulfilled the dream of an investor. A gorgeous second-story walk-up led gallery enthusiasts into an elegant art gallery that the village of Endicott could have only dreamed of. Everything had been refurbished, from the expansive hardwood flooring to state-of-the-art lighting.

My son, Professor Hall Groat II, was hired as the gallery director. Every exhibit installed was done in good taste and artists who represented the best the Southern Tier and surrounding regions had to offer were carefully selected. The openings were gala events with dinners and ballroom dancing to live music. Art lectures accompanied the shows, offering opportunities for students to mingle with professional artists. The gallery also provided the opportunity for collectors to meet the artists and learn firsthand what the creative mind had to offer society.

GRETCHEN LYNN GROAT

At five years old my daughter, Gretchen, displayed an unusual talent for composition with her series of small drawings and paintings. Today, her work has evolved into a sophisticated use of collage in mixed media paintings. Like many gifted artists, she won scholastic awards in high school, and by the time she graduated from Syracuse University, she was already showing in galleries. She exhibited in the Berkshires at the Tyringham Galleries with several one-person shows. The Munson-Williams-Proctor Arts Institute displayed her work for six years, which led to her popularity with collectors. Many galleries in Central New York have sold her work consisting of social commentaries. Gretchen's studies in psychology at Syracuse University are put to use, with an uncanny understanding of the human condition. The messages in her art are often subliminal, and the subject is not revealed immediately. Her color selections and composition are compelling to collectors and the mystery in her work gives it uniqueness. The New York Art Collection is proud to offer her work for sale.

A DOT WAS ADDED TO THE JACKSON POLLOCK

It was in the late 1940s. A few kids stood before the Syracuse museum's new acquisition of a Jackson Pollock modern masterpiece. This work was from a new series of Pollock's spatter paintings. The subject was brought up by one of the young students: "How would anyone know if a black dot was added?" After some discussion on the subject, one of the kids added a small black dot. This act of vandalism has never been detected and is forever lost in a maze of spatters and dribbles. The painting by Jackson Pollock and the mysterious dot is now worth millions and the additional dot has in no way altered the painting's greatness.

MERLIN PAINTED HIS WATERCOLORS
IN THE BATHTUB

One of my professors at Syracuse University was a very good watercolorist. His work was loose and free. He was rather quiet and withdrawn and what he once told me seemed out of character for such a serious man. Many years after my graduation, I asked Merlin how he watercolors in such a fluid way. He told me he does his watercolor painting in the bathtub. He was a tall and gangly man and I tried to visualize him in the tub with all his art equipment. Years later I told this story to my son. He said, "Dad, he was just pulling your leg—probably a joker." I took several courses from Merlin, and I do not recall him being anything other than serious. I believe he did paint his watercolors in the tub. Being an artist offers strange idiosyncrasies, and I assume we are all a little left of the norm.

MY MOTHER GAVE ME THIS BIRTHDAY GIFT, BUT WHO DID IT?

Five years ago I was hanging a large painting of a favorite local restaurant in a home in Cazenovia. My customer had some good sculpture and paintings and took an interest in each piece in his collection. Finally, he brought out a painting from another room and said it was his favorite impression of horses running through the tidal waters. He had no idea who painted it and wanted my input, as he hadn't noticed any signature. I directed his eye to the upper left-hand corner and had him read it. "Hall Groat," he said. "I had no idea this was by you, Hall. My mother gifted this to me a few years back, but I never realized it was by you. It's been my favorite painting, until now that you've hung this new work of the 'Seven Stone Steps.'"

ABRAHAM LINCOLN: AN IMPORTANT PAINTING

After painting a series of famous men over a twenty-year period, I believe one work stands out in front of all the rest. This 72-by-48-inch acrylic on canvas of Abraham Lincoln has been shown in a few exhibitions in the East, including a joint show with Hall Groat II at Cazenovia College. Lincoln is depicted as a somber, brooding man. However, the large head has tremendous impact and the viewer is drawn into this emotion-packed work. Terry Pickard, a collector of my work, owns this and several more of my paintings of oversized heads of famous people, including one of President Theodore Roosevelt. *Lincoln* may be his favorite in the series. By its mere size, it dominates the other portraits.

Lincoln
72 x 48 in. | Oil on canvas | By Hall Groat Sr.
Collection of Terry Pickard

MANLIUS PEBBLE HILL SCHOOL

As far back as I can remember The Manlius School was a prestigious military academy on Route 92, just over the hill from where I presently live. My sister went to some great dances there when she was a young girl and used to show me the school yearbook with cadets' autographs scrawled throughout. When the military academy merged with Pebble Hill School to form Manlius Pebble Hill School, it became an outstanding private school with a great heritage.

For the past several years my son and I have donated major paintings for its annual scholarship events. These have been sold at auction or silent auction. It is our small way of ensuring the great tradition continues. Each year my family attends the Pebble Hill Gala, a formal dinner dance, which was last held at the Turning Stone Casino.

New York City
30 x 40 in. | Oil on canvas | By Hall Groat Sr.

WASHINGTON PUB

Washington, D.C., was a great trip. I took my son, Hall, to the Smithsonian. At the National Portrait Museum, we saw the oil portrait of President Franklin Pierce, whose family we are related to. The National Galleries of Art, one of the world's finest museums, was the highlight of our trip. At the end of the day we spotted the Dubliner, an upscale pub in the center of D.C. and I went in costume. For fun I wore a priest's shirt and clerical collar. It's great to be away, as you never see anyone you know. While we were seated at a table, enjoying a mug of Guinness Stout, a friendly Irishman at a bar stool said, "Let me buy you and your young friend another drink, Father." "Why not, my son," I replied. He was inquisitive about my parish, so I had to avoid any conversation on this subject. He also asked if I had been to Coleman's Irish Pub in Syracuse. "Ya know, Father, up on Tipperary Hill." I replied, "Of course!" He then wanted me to meet the owner. At this point I got a little hot under my clerical collar. I was sure owner Peter Coleman knew me as a Syracuse artist, so I declined the meeting. Unbeknownst to me, Peter owned both pubs—Coleman's in Syracuse, as well as the Dubliner in D.C. The free booze suddenly stopped, as my little game became embarrassing. Of all the gin joints in all the towns all over the world, I walked into his!

RALPH MODELED FOR HIS PORTRAIT
STUDY IN ACRYLIC

There was a summer party at our house in Manlius. Ralph, our friend and neighbor, made great martinis and soon suggested we go into my studio and see if I could do an impression of him on canvas. Sometimes I accidentally dipped my brush into the martini I had set on my glass pallet. It didn't affect the flavor, other than adding a slight tonal change to the glass. Ralph was a good model and held still, although neither of us stopped talking. The distractions served as a means of relaxing the painter and the subject. I remember using a large brush so I could finish the painting quickly and not overwork it with too much detail. Miraculously, it came out quite well, which proved to me that a good martini is the prerequisite for a good painting.

Later I painted a liquor bottle still life that Ralph displayed for many years on his poolside patio in Sarasota. We had previously consumed the ingredients and this work had the same expressive qualities of his original portrait.

PAINTING SIGNED TWICE

In 1970, a couple who had acquired a large painting of mine called me from Austin, Texas. They said they were the highest bidder for this work at a New York auction house and that I hadn't signed it. They shipped it north to my studio and were exasperated with the whole expensive ordeal. When the crate arrived I saw my signature and found it hard to believe they hadn't seen it, even after I told them where to look. By luck I had a companion piece to this work. I called Austin and made a deal with them. If they looked at an image of a companion piece and also wanted it, I would send both of them back in the same crate. After I sent the image, they bought the companion piece and I took care of the return shipping for both pieces. I made no mention of their failure to see my signature, as I didn't want them to feel ignorant. I wonder if they ever realized I had now signed that work twice? Regardless, it turned out to be a good business decision for me.

FAN MAIL

Sometimes it's fun to look back at letters you have received from customers who have collected your work. Some people describe in great detail why they like your work, but more often, the letters are just a simple "thanks"—but in good taste. I put them in a file folder and enjoy re-reading them over the years. I suppose this makes me a sentimentalist, but it's a good idea to keep in contact with old customers because without them, where would you be? Many of my paintings are in honor of a birthday, wedding, anniversary or retirement of an executive. Sometimes a complete stranger writes about a painting of mine he happened to see on exhibit somewhere. The highest compliment you can receive is a montage painting of your entire life. I have painted many of these and they often have a lasting effect on a family. These paintings require photographic reference and a good working relationship with the people who commission them. The fan mail can lift an artist's spirits during those times when business is slow or you just can't remember a customer's name from years back.

DIVORCE SETTLEMENT: WHO GETS THE ART?

With the increasing amount of divorces, many couples fight over who gets the original art. I have had many customers pass this dilemma by me and I always suggest they purchase a current appraisal. My son, Professor Hall Groat II, handles all appraisals of my work. He is the most qualified and is also now my leading dealer. There are many qualified art appraisers, but through the years, even the best have ended up calling me for help in establishing the value of an artwork. Everyone who owns original art by a qualified professional artist should have it appraised. Divorce is too often an emotional time in life, and it's good to have peace of mind. In estate planning you should also consider the sentimental attachments to the art collection, which can often be more important than the intrinsic value.

The Hindu
24 x 24 in. | Oil on panel | By Hall Groat Sr.

THE CANADIAN DISCOVERY

Recently, I received an e-mail from a Canadian couple, with an attachment of a watercolor by me. It was a wedding gift from their parents who were now deceased. The parents had said it was purchased in Oakland, California, where they lived when they were first married. The Canadian couple had no idea who the parents had purchased it from. I have relatives living in that part of California, but so far, my attempts to find anyone who may have owned it have been futile.

It may always remain a mystery. Nevertheless, I was elated to see this photo image after so many years. Artwork has a way of surfacing in unexpected ways.

THE *TITANIC* IN BUDAPEST

An e-mail message arrived a few years ago from Hungary. A collector attached an image of my painting of the *Titanic* next to an iceberg. He told me he bought it on eBay from a party in Baldwinsville, New York. I remembered painting a 90th birthday surprise for a man who remembered the *Titanic* and had lost a relative on it. When he died it went into an estate that was sold off, and the picture ended up in Budapest. The Hungarian collector, Tanito, bought a few more of my works, but the *Titanic* was always his favorite.

SPRINGFIELD NATIONAL ART EXHIBITION: PRIDE IN REJECTION

The director of the George Walter Vincent Smith Art Museum in Springfield, Massachusetts, was disgusted with the jury for the art exhibition that year in the 1960s. The good art was thrown out in favor of the judge's distorted perception of what constituted good. A separate exhibition, featuring many of the rejects, was installed on the museum's third floor. When the art reviewer came to cover the show, the accepted work on the second floor was panned, but many of the rejected pieces received rave reviews. I took pride in my rejection, which won a purchase award several years later, and became part of the permanent collection at Cooperstown Museum.

NEIGHBORS FISHING THROUGH TRASH

Moving from one apartment to another seems to be a way of life when you're young. When you're an artist, there is always an accumulation of sketches, studies, or doodles that collect. You can't keep storing everything, so you usually have to weed out the best to move to that new location. It's not unusual to be forced to discard work you have determined isn't up to your level. I've had people admit to rummaging through my trash in search of that special drawing. With the new movement called "Freeganism" taking place around the world, materialism is frowned upon. Foraging through dumpsters, Freeganists may discover some surprising artworks, as well as edible food discarded from restaurants.

When I was living in a rooming house, my landlady discovered a box full of art I had left in her garage. Forty-some years later she called me to say the biggest mistake in her life was tossing it in the trash. My work had appreciated in that time and she could have made some serious money. You can discover many surprises by fishing through an artist's trash, unless the work has been shredded.

PAINE–WEBBER AND THE FOOT CONTEST

The brokerage firm of Paine-Webber invited me to a party after it moved to a new location. Henry Wildhack, one of my customers, was talking to me about investments in art and Syracuse sports, when he introduced me to Judge Neal McCurn. After a few martinis, the subject of sore feet came up. I told the judge I had perfect feet and after two years in the infantry as a foot soldier, never once had a sore foot. It became one-upmanship, as the judge went on to say he had the best feet and was sure they were more streamlined than mine. After another sip of my martini, I told the judge that, aesthetically, his feet could be no match for mine. Henry suggested Neal and I should "put our feet where our mouth is." The whole office watched as Judge McCurn and I removed our shoes and socks for the democratic vote. The judge was a shoe-in and walked away the victor. I like to think it was politics at play, but the judge did have great looking feet.

Amsterdam Drawbridge
24 x 36 in. | Oil on panel | By Hall Groat Sr.

COUNTY ROAD GANG

One summer, when I was a Nottingham High School student, I worked on the road gang for the county. We patched roads with hot tar and covered them with gravel. There was a group of kids from Valley High that I enjoyed working with. The soft job was moving the truck along, but I found the brakes were bad as it rolled forward and elected to stay behind the truck with the tar and gravel spreaders. Getting hired was based on knowing some politician. I had a buddy whose father held an influential office. I didn't realize it at the time, but working on county roads familiarized me with the subject matter I was later to paint pictures of. We patched roads in the Pompey hills and the view was exhilarating. The great wide vista of Syracuse, Onondaga Lake and Oneida Lake was inspiring to me even at that young age.

BANK EXECUTIVE WIFE NEEDED REASSURANCE

It's hard to be the wife of a powerful bank CEO. Mable was in an uncomfortable position at the opening of the annual regional exhibition. After all, it was her husband's bank that awarded the grand prize. The painting was beyond her comprehension and she wanted to represent her husband as a woman in the know. Mable remembered me, as I was the paperboy in her neighborhood ten years earlier. She cornered me in the exhibition hall and was looking for reassurance. Mable asked me if the grand prize oil was supposed to be good. I suggested she ask the artist, who was standing nearby. Frank was my illustration teacher at Syracuse University. She knew enough not to ask him, but wanted to compliment him on his award. Finally, after a glass or two of wine, she went ahead and complimented him over the public address system: "On behalf of Syracuse's oldest bank we offer our sincere congratulations on your great painting, Frank." Later she took me aside and informed me this work of art lacked the anguish of a struggling artist and seemed dated. She was sure it should not have won. I asked Mable how she came up with this deduction and told her I thought it was an outstanding piece. She told me she overheard two art professors say this by the punch bowl. As the wife of a powerful bank executive, she had to appear in the know. "And why didn't you inform me it was supposed to be good, Hally?" I told her she came up with a more informed decision on her own. She always tried hard to say what would further her husband's career. If she didn't, she would hear about it at home.

THE MOST EXTRAORDINARY STUDENT I'VE EVER HAD

When I was about forty years old, there was a period of time I gave private art lessons. An elderly gentleman's wife called and asked if I would give her husband lessons. She may have wanted him out of the house for awhile, as she was his caregiver and needed a break. The eighty-eight-year-old loved nautical scenes and had spent years yachting in New England. On the day of his first lesson he arrived with a folder of references on famous yachts, including many he had sailed in America's Cup races. When I began my instruction on how to compose a painting, he politely informed me he had his own way of working and was more interested in showing me his method. When I introduced him to ways of mixing colors for his painting, he informed me he had spent years developing his own system and wanted to show me everything he had learned about color. When he started painting, it was obvious he had studied art, but was still an amateur. After coming to my studio for several months, it was apparent he just wanted my company and wanted to share his knowledge about nautical art. I was very interested in his stories of being at sea in the North Atlantic and always looked forward to his visits. The only thing I was unable to do was teach him how to be a better painter. The old gentleman really didn't come to learn; he was only interested in teaching what he knew and attempted to reverse roles with me. Perhaps he was beyond an age when you're receptive to new ideas. When he was showing me how he paints, he was the happiest. Finally, one day his wife informed me he had to discontinue his lessons, but said those visits to my studio had brought him great joy. He passed away soon after. He was an extraordinary person, and as his teacher I became the beneficiary of his years of instruction, as well as his experiences in yachting.

CAZENOVIA COLLEGE
LE CHEVAL

In November 2010, I was invited to submit a series of paintings for an exhibition of horse paintings at the Cazenovia College Art Gallery in Reisman Hall. In the show were works by some of the best horse painters in the U.S.A. and Canada. The exhibition covered many styles and various ways of interpreting the horse, from polo pony to racetrack. It seemed important for me to introduce new work that dealt with the horse in a way rarely seen. My subject was air rescue by helicopter from a runaway forest fire in the West. It illustrated the way brave forest rangers and helicopter pilots risk their lives to save many horses from being incinerated in a wildfire. Every year there are literally thousands lost in these infernos. I gave a gallery talk on this subject and discussed the complexity of my painting.

Air Rescue
70 x 48 in. | Oil on canvas | By Hall Groat Sr.
Le Cheval, Group Exhibition
Cazenovia College Art Gallery, Reisman Hall

CUSTOMER IN SPAIN

September 2010 marked my largest sale on record to an individual customer overseas. Following an initial order of a painting a customer in Spain fell in love with, my son, Hall Groat II, handled the order for an additional twenty-five of my oil paintings. We encouraged the Spaniard to try one work first to see how he liked it. It was a brilliant move by my son and business partner. Communication was difficult as our new customer spoke no English, and my son had to translate messages about all details from color, sizes and shipping instructions. The Spaniard used so much jargon it often became a guessing game as to what he was asking. Shipping alone was nearly one thousand dollars after we spent no less than thirteen hours packing the art. You must be insightful to put together an order of this size, especially when it's for a major international collector. Negotiations take patience and you must be prepared to give a package price, as well as deal with a counter offer. The whole deal could fall apart at any moment. We had the Spaniard pick up the shipping cost and sold all work unframed. It was an unusual request, but we had to throw in twenty-five brass title plaques to accompany each work to clinch the deal. Our new customer had several homes and preferred to display his collections in a formal way. With the weakening dollar, many European collectors have been buying American art—and finding a new market is important.

IF I COULD GO WHERE MY PAINTINGS GO

Much of my work is sold directly from my studio or through galleries around the country. Some of my paintings are with me for years, while others are sold a few days after completion. It often leaves me with that empty studio syndrome when so much of my art has left me for good. Many paintings end up in gorgeous homes and offices. Some are the subject of conversations at penthouse parties that rarely include me on the guest list. A few of my works are even fought over in divorce court. The paintings must stand alone and I can no longer speak for them. Questions arise like, "Wonder who the artist is or if he's still living?" or "Where is his signature?" I'm happy for the painting's success, but admit to being a bit jealous. I rarely get to go where my paintings go or share in their lifestyle. Then again, my paintings may not remember me, as I was much younger when they were created.

Homestead Remembered
24 x 30 in. | Oil on canvas | By Hall Groat Sr.

Hall Groat II and Hall Groat Sr. discussing a painting.

DEALING WITH THE QUESTION

Twenty years ago I was going down the elevator in MONY towers with one of my longtime best customers who was head of the Mutual of New York Syracuse office. He made a curious statement: "Hall, I have collected about thirty of your best paintings over the past seven years and I have had trouble deciding whether you're a great painter or a great businessman." After years of thinking about that statement—if I was a great painter or a great businessman—I was ready to deal with it. My son and I have a successful online business and have developed an international customer base that is growing every day. He runs the business with his computer skills and understands every aspect of the business. He's a world-class realist painter as well. When I look at how far my personal sales reach around the globe, I have come to a conclusion. My art must stand alone because new buyers in many countries are less familiar with me and the work must speak for itself. If it sells, it has done so on its own merit.

That's only half of the answer to the question my friend asked. The "great businessman" part of the question is even more complex to answer. I've been in sales and barter all my life and have had fun doing it since I was four years old. I admit when I close a deal it still gives me a high. My father, Romaine, had a fabulous personality and his customers often bought his products whether they needed them or not. When I was a kid I went on a few business trips with him and watched how he interacted with customers. He had a reputation as a great self-employed salesman. He died at fifty-nine while I was away in the service. I inherited some of his business acumen and applied it to my career as an artist. Selling direct is the most rewarding thing I do and that personal contact with customers is important to me. *I think this indicates that I am a good artist and a good businessman*—QUESTION ANSWERED!

ABOUT THE AUTHOR

Although Hall Groat Sr. is best known for his impressionistic paintings that are in collections internationally, his love for writing has consumed much of his time for the past fifteen years. Many of his works consist of vignettes, essays and poetry. In 2009, Groat had the lead story in a collection of works published by Mel Rubenstein titled *The Peacetime Draft During the Cold War*. The Syracuse Symphony Orchestra published in its quarterly programs several of Groat's works based on his brief encounters with maestros Leopold Stokowski, Arthur Fiedler, and Sir Michael Tippett of the London symphony. Many letters have been published in *The Post-Standard* in recent years that deal with domestic and political issues.